20 Reading Comprehension Games

Marla Love

Teacher, North Albany Grade School
Albany, Oregon

D1561194

A FEARON
MAKEMASTER® BOOK

DAVID S. LAKE PUBLISHERS, Belmont, California

Edited by Beverly Cory
Designed by Paul Quin
Art by John Hammett, Gustavo Medina, and Paul Quin

ISBN-0-8224-5800-4

Printed in the United States of America.

Introduction   iv

1 Following Directions

2 Finding Details

3 Finding Main Idea

4 Drawing Conclusions

5 Locating Information

6 Distinguishing Fact from Opinion

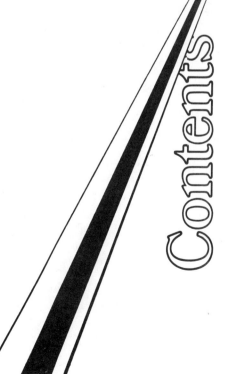

Exciting reading games add interest and spice to all types of reading and language arts programs. The games in this book, developed and classroom-tested with fourth, fifth, and sixth graders, provide practice in six important comprehension skills: following directions, finding details, finding main idea, drawing conclusions, locating information, and distinguishing fact from opinion.

These games can be adapted to a variety of learning situations. They are effective when used every day during reading time with small groups of two to four students. Each player's responses are checked by the other players or by a game leader, providing immediate reinforcement and maximum learning.

In addition, the games may be made available in a reading learning center for independent use when assignments are completed. Or, you may duplicate multiple copies of the games and give each student his own copy to color, mount, and take home to play with family and friends.

The approximate grade level of each game appears in the table of contents. This should not limit the use of any game, however. The games have been used successfully with both advanced students and slow learners in all the intermediate grades, and can be adjusted for use at any grade level.

The twenty games included in this book are easy to assemble and use. Eighteen involve a game board, some with correlated cards; two are simply card games. When you decide to use a game, just duplicate the appropriate pages and let the students do the rest. They can cut apart the cards and tape together the two-page game boards or mount them on a single large sheet. They may also color any of the items to add brightness and a personal touch to each game.

You may want to laminate the materials for extra durability. First mount the game boards and cards on construction paper or lightweight tagboard, then run them through a laminator, or encase them in clear contact paper or acetate.

Game markers for the players can be pop bottle caps, small race cars, colored plastic paper clips, or similar small objects. Games based on newspaper clippings or library file cards can be supplemented with items collected or prepared by your students.

Most of the games require the use of a single ordinary die or a six-space spinner. A sample spinner is provided at the end of this book. You may duplicate several spinners and have them colored and laminated, like the other materials, for added durability and attractiveness.

The purpose of each game, the suggested number of players, and the materials needed are listed with the game rules. For quick reference, keep each set of rules with the appropriate game board and cards, storing them together in an envelope or folder labeled with the game title.

Introduction

1

Following Directions

Excursion

Purpose   To follow directions based on a street map.

Number of players   2–4

Materials   Excursion game board
Errand cards
Single die or spinner
Marker for each player

Rules   1   Each player in turn rolls the die or spins and moves
his marker the number of spaces shown.
2   If a player lands on an Errand space, he draws an
Errand card and follows the directions.
3   If a player lands on an intersection, he must take the
side road either forward or backward.
4   The first player to reach school is the winner.

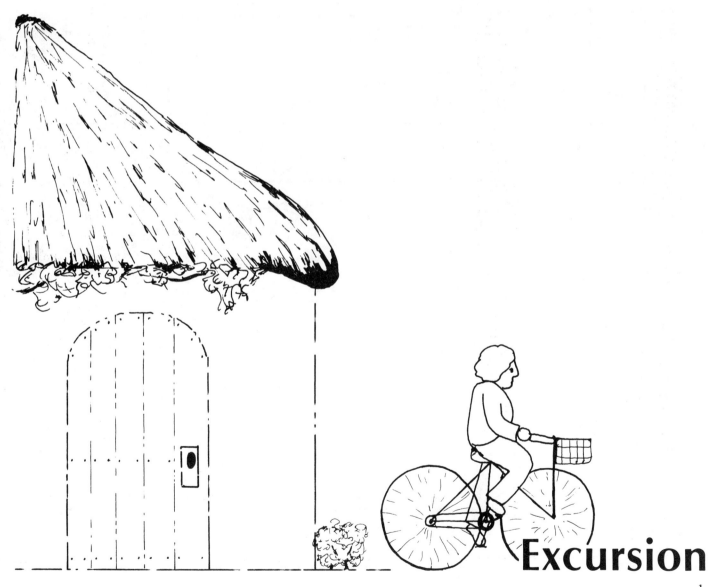

Excursion

Excursion

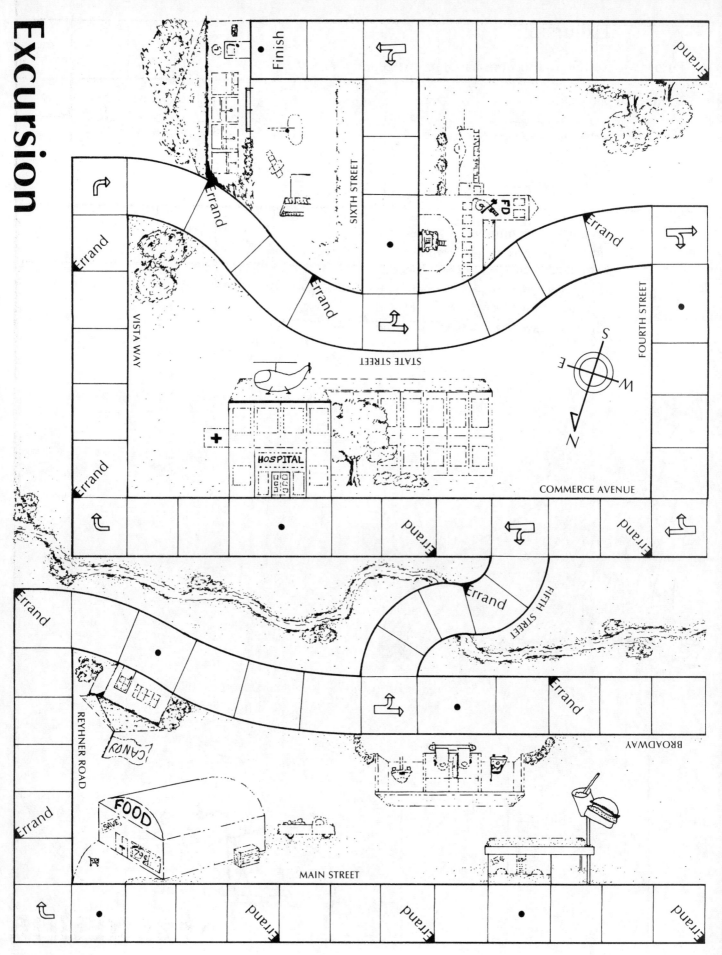

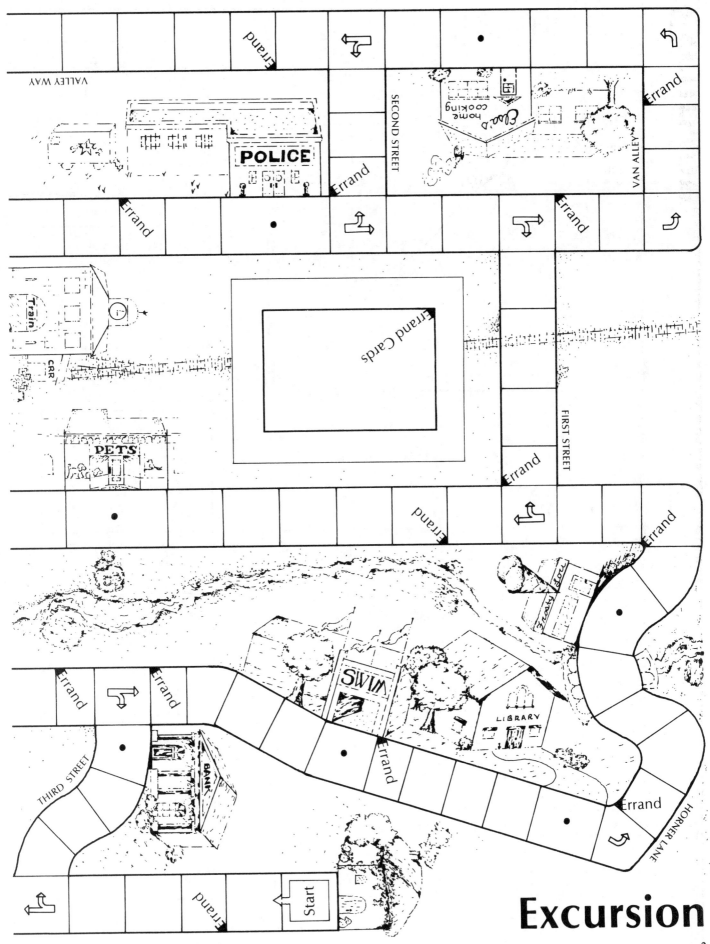

VALLEY WAY

POLICE

Ella's home cooking

SECOND STREET

VAN ALLEY

Errand

Errand

Errand

Errand

Errand

Errand

Errand Cards

Train

CRR

PETS

FIRST STREET

Errand

Errand

Errand

Errand

Errand

Errand

SWIM

LIBRARY

Errand

THIRD STREET

BANK

Errand

HORNER LANE

Errand

Start

Excursion

3

Excursion

Move to candy store. Then move west 3 spaces.

Errand

Move to hospital. Then move east 2 spaces.

Errand

Move to burger stand. Then move west 5 spaces.

Errand

Move to service station. Then move west 4 spaces.

Errand

Move to train station. Then move north 3 spaces.

Errand

Move to bank. Then move north 2 spaces.

Errand

Move to library. Then move west 1 space, and south 3 spaces.

Errand

Move to police station. Then move east 7 spaces.

Errand

Move to supermarket. Then move west 2 spaces.

Errand

Move to ice cream parlor. Then move south 2 spaces, and east 4 spaces.

Errand

Move to restaurant. Then move east 3 spaces.

Errand

Move to swimming pool. Then move east 2 spaces.

Errand

Move to pet store. Then move east 1 space.

Errand

Move to fire station. Then move north 1 space, and west 3 spaces.

Errand

Speedway

Purpose   To follow directions based on geometric shapes,
measurement, and the alphabet.

Number of players   2–4

Materials   Speedway game board
Single die or spinner
Marker for each player
Pencil, paper, ruler

Rules   1   Each player in turn rolls the die or spins and moves
his marker the number of spaces shown.
2   To stay where he lands, the player must correctly
follow the direction in that space.
3   If the player does not follow the direction correctly,
he must return to his previous position.
4   If a player lands on Pit Stop, he loses one turn.
5   Play continues with the players racing five times
around the Speedway. The first player to complete
the fifth lap is the winner.

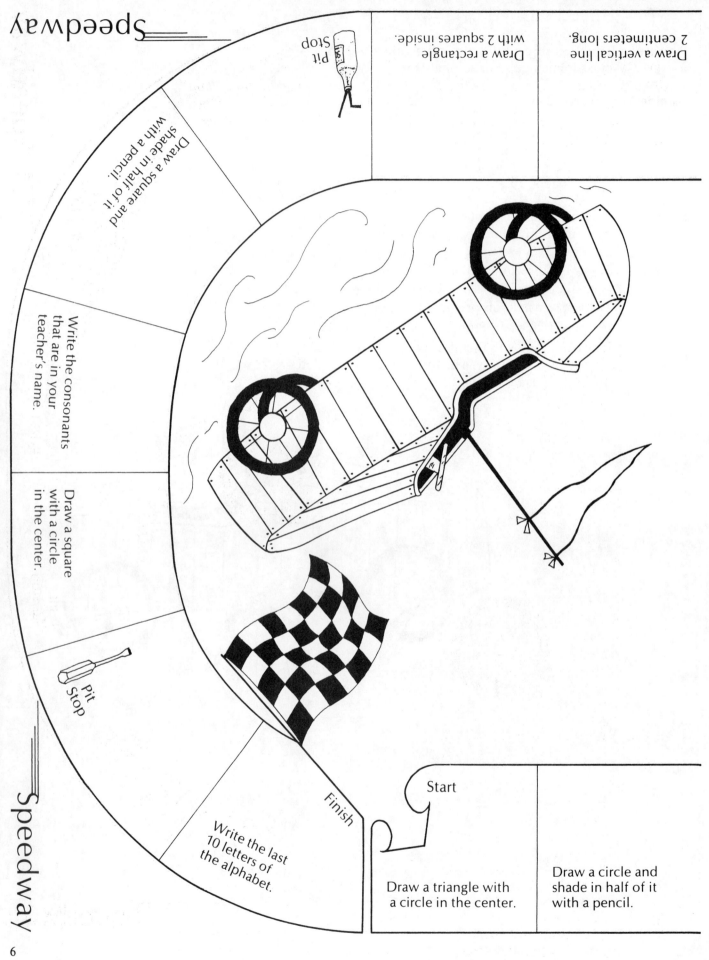

Speedway

Draw a vertical line 2 centimeters long.

Draw a rectangle with 2 squares inside.

Pit Stop

Draw a square and shade in half of it with a pencil.

Write the consonants that are in your teacher's name.

Draw a square with a circle in the center.

Pit Stop

Write the last 10 letters of the alphabet.

Finish

Start

Draw a triangle with a circle in the center.

Draw a circle and shade in half of it with a pencil.

Speedway

6

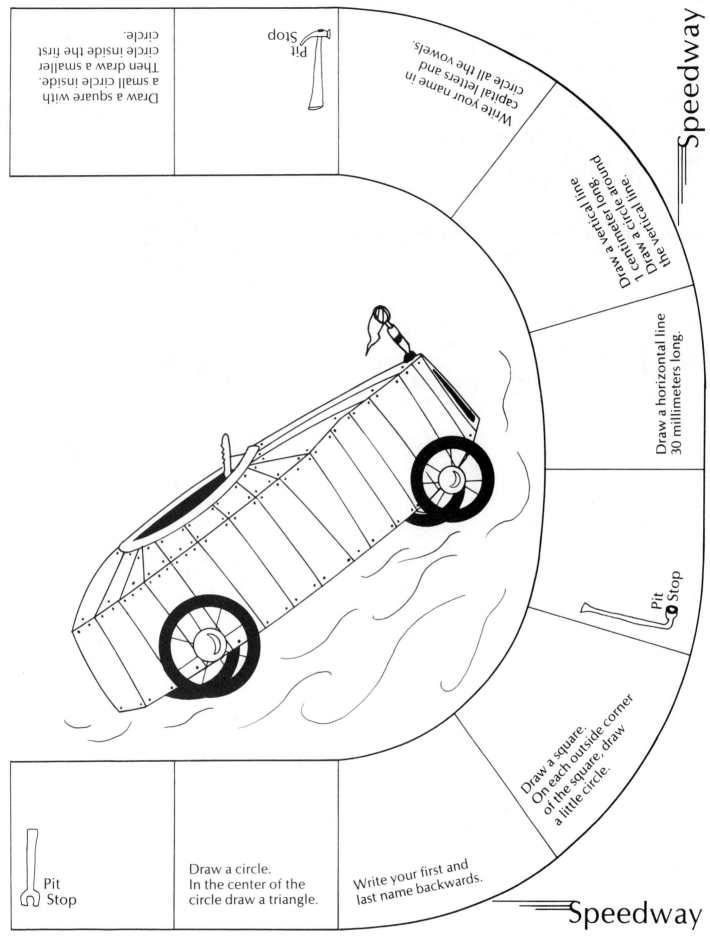

Write your name in capital letters and circle all the vowels.

Pit Stop

Draw a square with a small circle inside. Then draw a smaller circle inside the first circle.

Draw a vertical line 1 centimeter long. Draw a circle around the vertical line.

Draw a horizontal line 30 millimeters long.

Pit Stop

Draw a square. On each outside corner of the square, draw a little circle.

Pit Stop

Draw a circle. In the center of the circle draw a triangle.

Write your first and last name backwards.

Speedway

7

Diamond Mine

Purpose   To follow directions based on numerical and geometric terms.

Number of players   2–4

Materials   Diamond Mine game board
            Diamond cards
            Single die or spinner
            Marker for each player
            Pencil, paper

Rules   1 Each player in turn rolls the die or spins and moves his marker the number of spaces shown.
        2 To stay where he lands, the player must correctly follow the direction on that space.
        3 If the player does not follow the direction correctly, he must return to his previous position.
        4 If a player lands on a Diamond space, he draws a Diamond card and follows the direction.
        5 The first player to reach the Diamond Heap is the winner.

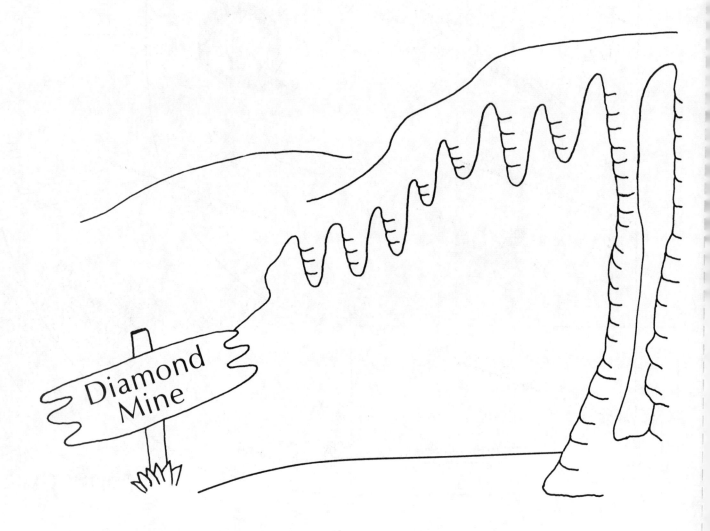

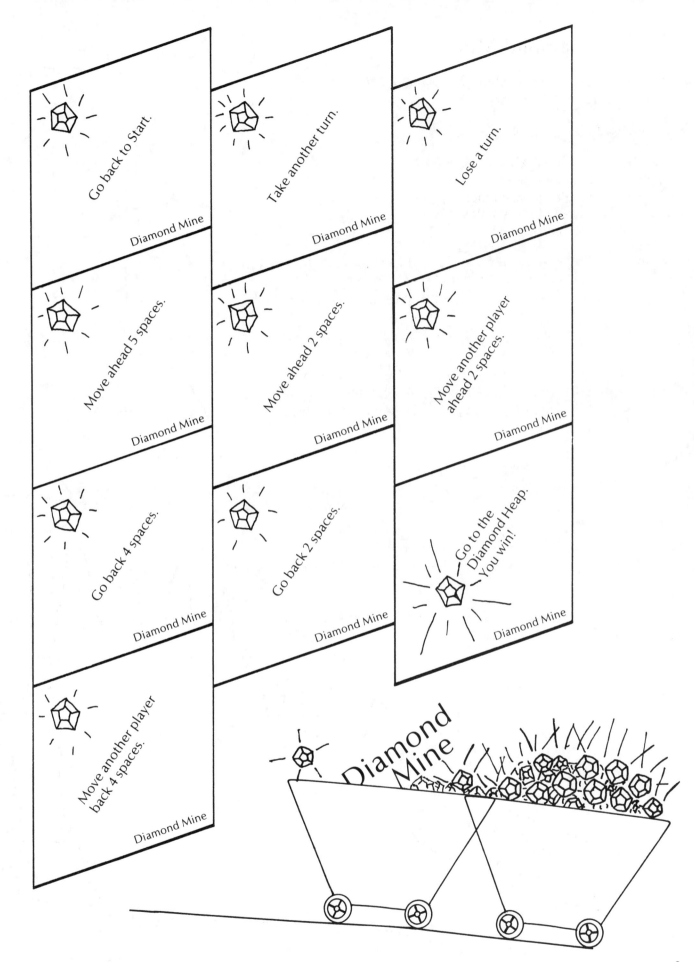

Go back to Start.

Diamond Mine

Take another turn.

Diamond Mine

Lose a turn.

Diamond Mine

Move ahead 5 spaces.

Diamond Mine

Move ahead 2 spaces.

Diamond Mine

Move another player ahead 2 spaces.

Diamond Mine

Go back 4 spaces.

Diamond Mine

Go back 2 spaces.

Diamond Mine

Go to the Diamond Heap. You win!

Diamond Mine

Move another player back 4 spaces.

Diamond Mine

Diamond Mine

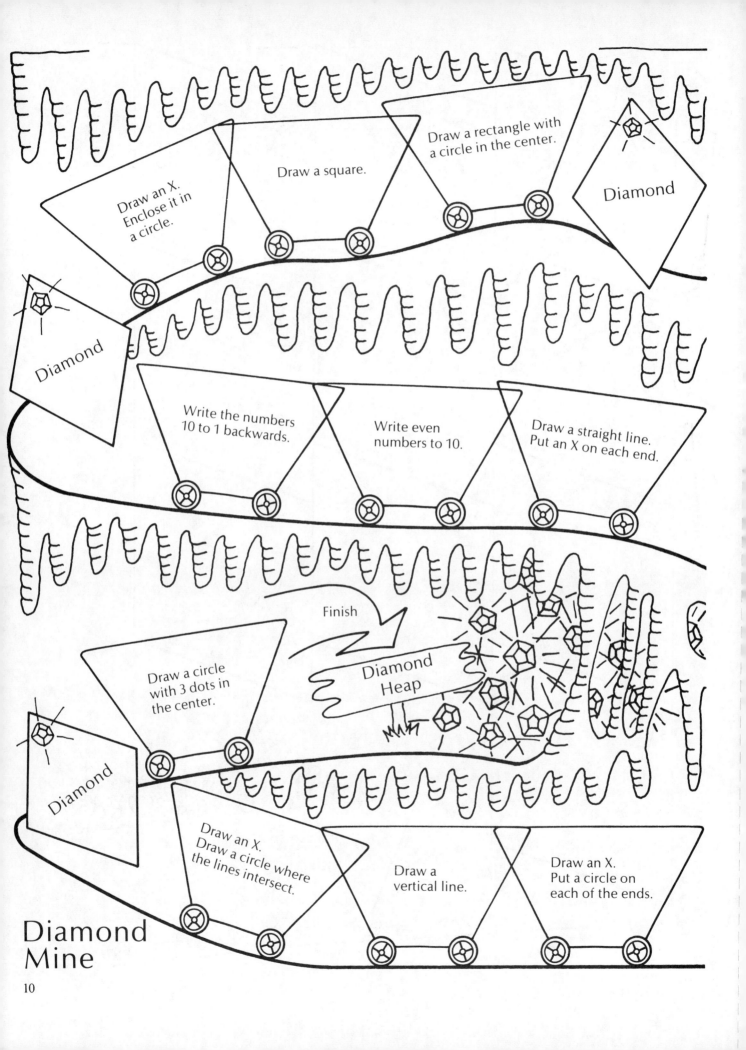

Draw an X. Enclose it in a circle.

Draw a square.

Draw a rectangle with a circle in the center.

Diamond

Diamond

Write the numbers 10 to 1 backwards.

Write even numbers to 10.

Draw a straight line. Put an X on each end.

Finish

Diamond Heap

Draw a circle with 3 dots in the center.

Diamond

Draw an X. Draw a circle where the lines intersect.

Draw a vertical line.

Draw an X. Put a circle on each of the ends.

Diamond Mine

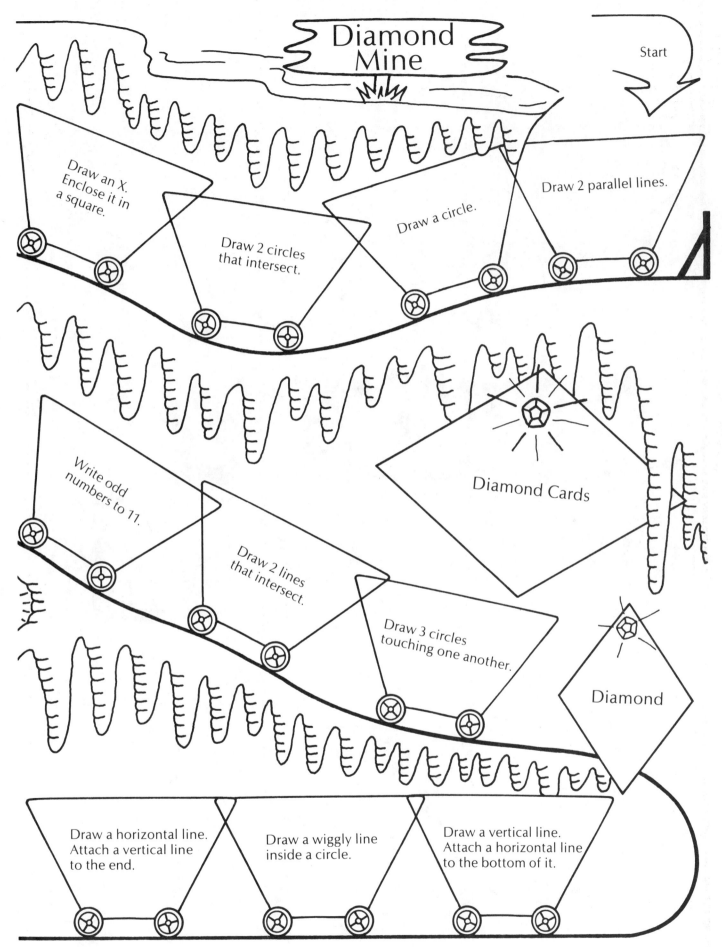

Diamond
Mine

Start

Draw an X. Enclose it in a square.

Draw 2 circles that intersect.

Draw a circle.

Draw 2 parallel lines.

Write odd numbers to 11.

Draw 2 lines that intersect.

Diamond Cards

Draw 3 circles touching one another.

Diamond

Draw a horizontal line. Attach a vertical line to the end.

Draw a wiggly line inside a circle.

Draw a vertical line. Attach a horizontal line to the bottom of it.

Witchcraft

Purpose To follow directions based on numerical computations.

Number of players 2–4

Materials Witchcraft game board
Single die or spinner
Marker for each player
Pencil, paper

Rules
1 Each player in turn rolls the die or spins and moves his marker the number of spaces shown.
2 To stay where he lands, the player must correctly follow the direction on that space.
3 If the player does not follow the direction correctly, he must move back to the nearest Spider's Tooth.
4 The first player to reach the Slimy Serpent is the winner.

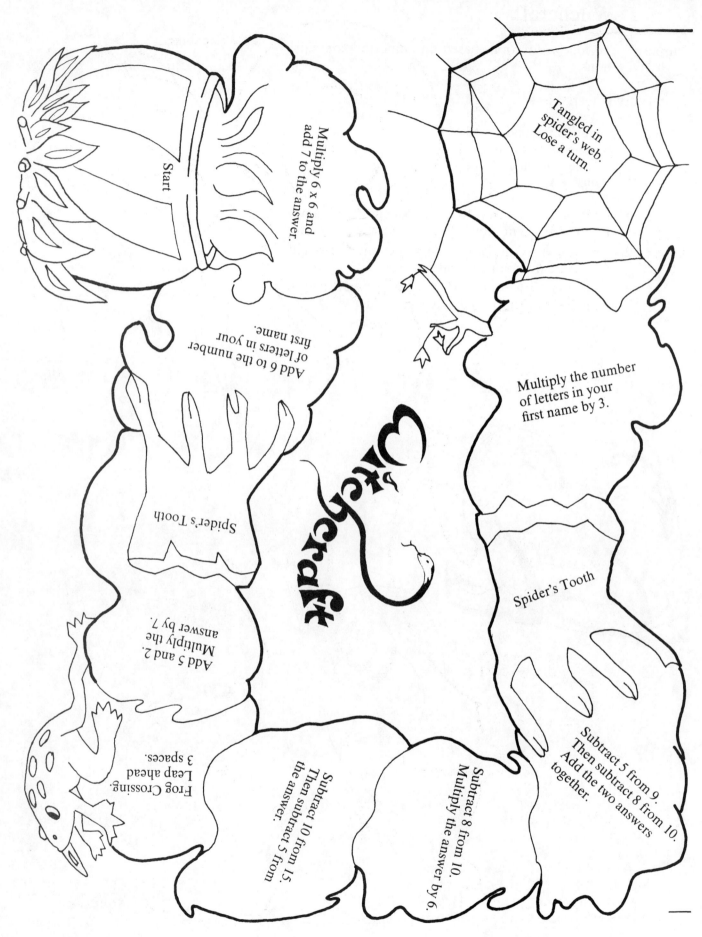

Start

Multiply 6 x 6 and add 7 to the answer.

Add 6 to the number of letters in your first name.

Spider's Tooth

Add 5 and 2. Multiply the answer by 7.

Frog Crossing. Leap ahead 3 spaces.

Subtract 10 from 15. Then subtract 5 from

Subtract 8 from 10. Multiply the answer by 6.

Subtract 5 from 9. Then subtract 8 from 10. Add the two answers together.

Spider's Tooth

Multiply the number of letters in your first name by 3.

Tangled in spider's web. Lose a turn.

Witchcraft

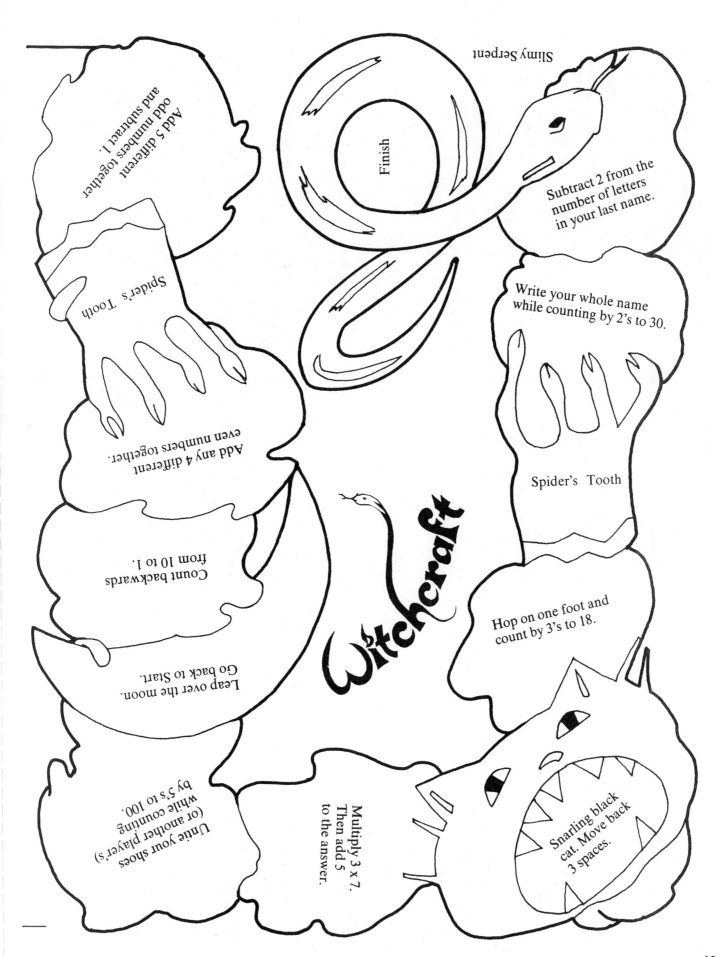

Slimy Serpent

Finish

Add 5 different odd numbers together and subtract 1.

Spider's Tooth

Subtract 2 from the number of letters in your last name.

Write your whole name while counting by 2's to 30.

Add any 4 different even numbers together.

Spider's Tooth

Count backwards from 10 to 1.

Witchcraft

Leap over the moon. Go back to Start.

Hop on one foot and count by 3's to 18.

Untie your shoes (or another player's) while counting by 5's to 100.

Multiply 3 x 7. Then add 5 to the answer.

Snarling black cat. Move back 3 spaces.

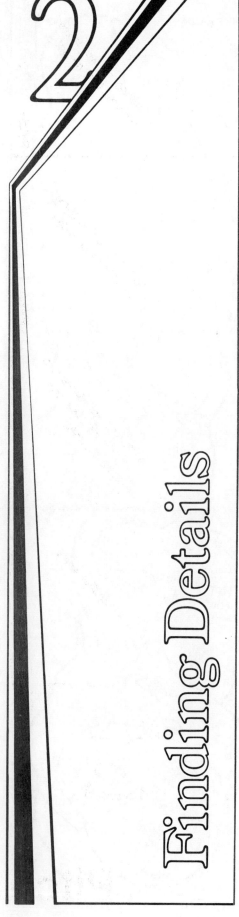

Finding Details

Pitch

Purpose   To find and recall details from a story that all the players have read.

Number of players   2–4

Materials   Pitch game board
Pitch cards
Story from reading book
Single die or spinner
Marker for each player

Rules   1   Play begins at home plate. Each player in turn rolls the die or spins and moves his marker the number of spaces shown.

2   To stay where he lands, the player must correctly answer the question on that space.

3   If a player cannot answer correctly, he must return his marker to its previous position.

4   If a player lands on a Pitch space, he draws a card and follows the directions. The player moves ahead two spaces if he responds correctly and moves back one space if he responds incorrectly.

5   Players score one run each time they pass home plate. The first player to score five runs is the winner.

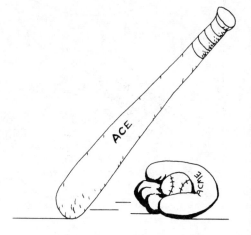

Run to 2nd base. Do not cross home plate. **Pitch**	Find a word that describes the setting. **Pitch**	Run to 3rd base. Do not cross home plate. **Pitch**	Choose two words and tell what they mean. **Pitch**
Find two words that describe the main character. **Pitch**	Hit a home run. Go to home plate and score 1 point. **Pitch**	Name a character you would not like for a friend. Why? **Pitch**	Find a word that shows someone was happy. **Pitch**
Run to 1st base. Do not cross home plate. **Pitch**	How was the main problem solved? **Pitch**	Find a descriptive phrase. **Pitch**	Bases loaded. Home run. Go to home plate and score 4 points. **Pitch**
What was the main problem? **Pitch**	Find five descriptive words. **Pitch**	Strike 3. Go to home plate. No point. **Pitch**	Find a negative word. **Pitch**
Find three words that begin with the letter r. Tell what they mean. **Pitch**	Fly ball! You're out! Go to home plate. No point. **Pitch**		

Pitch

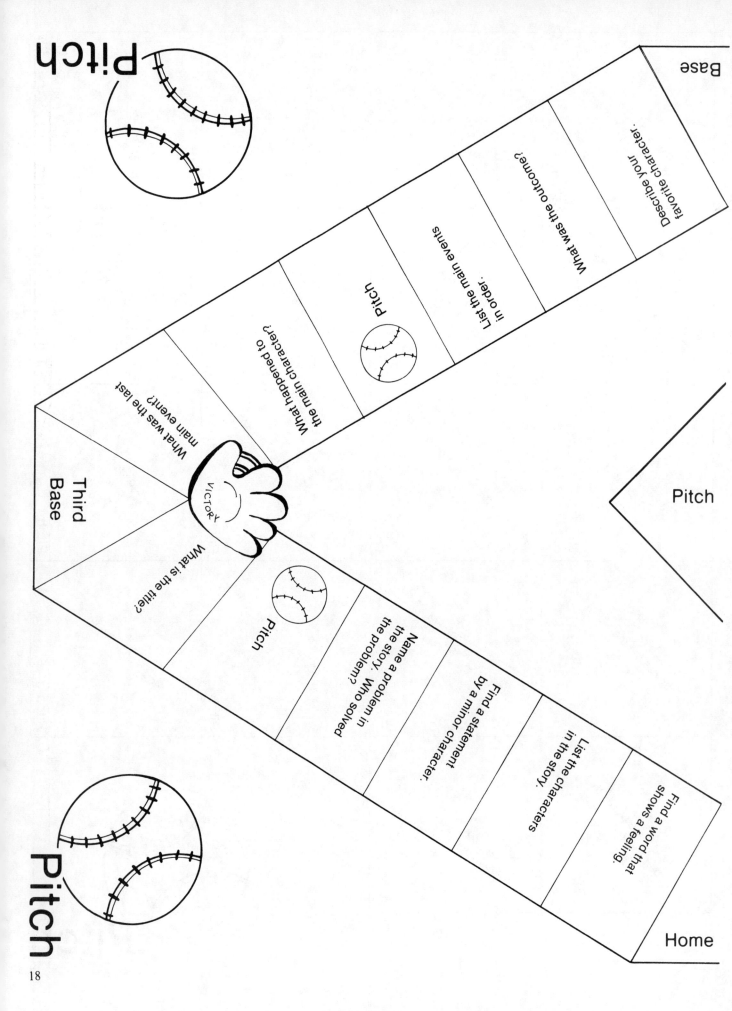

Pitch

Base

Describe your favorite character.

What was the outcome?

List the main events in order.

Pitch

What happened to the main character?

What was the last main event?

Third Base

What is the title?

VICTORY

Pitch

Name a problem in the story. Who solved the problem?

Find a statement by a minor character.

List the characters in the story.

Find a word that shows a feeling.

Pitch

Home

18

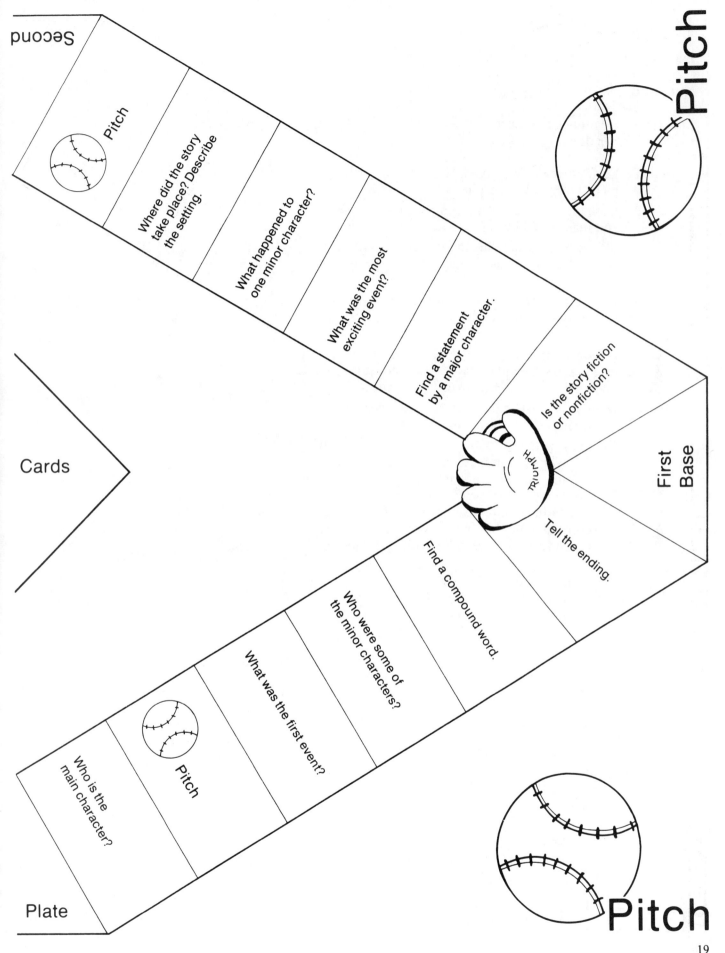

Second

Pitch

Where did the story take place? Describe the setting.

What happened to one minor character?

What was the most exciting event?

Find a statement by a major character.

Is the story fiction or nonfiction?

Tell the ending.

First Base

Find a compound word.

Who were some of the minor characters?

What was the first event?

Pitch

Who is the main character?

Plate

Cards

TRIUMPH

Pitch

Pitch

19

Headliner

Purpose   Reading for details in news articles.

Number of players   3

Materials   Headliner headlines
Headliner articles

Rules

1. Each player is dealt five headlines. The articles are placed facedown in a pile.
2. Each player in turn draws an article from the pile and reads it to himself.
3. If the player has the headline that goes with the article drawn, he has a matched pair which he lays down faceup. This completes his turn.
4. If the player does not have the matching headline, he briefly summarizes the article and asks a specific player for the correct headline.
5. If the player asked has the correct headline, he must give it away. The player who asked for it now has a matched pair and may take another turn.
6. If the player asked does not have the correct headline, the article is placed at the bottom of the pile.
7. Challenge:
   a. A player who disagrees with the match of a headline and article may challenge.
   b. If the match is incorrect, the challenger wins the headline and one extra turn. The article is returned to the bottom of the pile.
   c. If the match is correct, the challenger loses one turn.
8. Play continues until all headlines and articles are matched. The winner is the player with the most matched pairs.

Headliner

Beaked Whale Found Beached

Headliner

Rainers Score

Headliner

Monster Seen In Loch Ness

Headliner

A beaked whale, one of the rarest specimens roaming waters off the Pacific coast, washed ashore Saturday at Newport.

The whale was 15 to 18 feet long.

Tests will be performed on the whale's skull to determine its age. The valuable skull will be sent to a museum.

Headliner

After trailing 0–1 in the eighth inning, the Rainers came back and notched a 3–1 baseball victory over the Lakers.

The win pushes the Rainers into first place in the league standings.

The Rainers will try to maintain their lead when they play the Wildcats in a league game at Federal Way on Friday.

Headliner

Two dark-colored fins about 20 feet apart were seen moving rapidly through the waters of Loch Ness in Scotland. The lake in between the fins bubbled and swirled, creating the illusion of boiling water. The fins submerged completely, then resurfaced, then submerged again, sending a tremendous wave sweeping toward the shore.

Headliner

Bee Flight —By Jet!

Headliner

The airline passengers departed routinely when their flight landed. But their baggage and a swarm of angry bees stayed aboard.

The bees had been confined in containers for shipment. But when baggage workers opened the hold, the compartment was filled with a swarm of angry bees.

Headliner

Headliner

Farmer Tells of Strange Visitors

Dorothy Wins!

Deaf Teen Reads Lips

It was 3:30 A.M. and farmer John Smith was milking the cows when suddenly the barn lights went out. He found a flashlight, went outside, and saw a glowing saucer-shaped object hovering over his barn.

He said the object was 80 feet long, 30 feet high, noiseless, and covered with lots of small windows in rows.

The startled farmer watched the object until it suddenly shot straight up and merged with the stars.

Game! Set! Match! Dorothy Brown defeated last year's champion Betty Gillam 6–4, 6–3 in the Lorenz Tennis Tournament.

Dorothy, who first picked up a tennis racket only three years ago, has become an accomplished player.

She will meet National Champion Lil Cristen next week in the Shearer Tournament.

Joan Jones is a high school sophomore who watches you intently and flashes a ready smile as you talk to her.

Not all her friends realize that since June, Joan has been deaf.

"Going deaf doesn't bother me, as long as I can read lips," she says matter-of-factly. "People go through it."

Joan is so good at lip reading that her handicap is invisible until someone speaks without first catching her attention.

Headliner

Police rushed to the city's middle school Saturday after an alarmed caller reported hearing gunshots behind the building.

The officers stayed to watch the remainder of the track meet in progress.

Shot Fools Caller

New Radar Gun Gets Speeders

Headliner

Dog Denied Vote

Headliner

Brakes Fail— Bus Cleans Up

Headliner

If you took the last corner a little fast, do not be surprised if you spot a motorcycle policeman pointing an ominous, black-barreled gun at you.

If that sounds scary, it should— but not because the police are pointing weapons at motorists. There is no danger of being shot. The gun is a radar device designed to catch speeders.

Headliner

Guzzy Garrison, a registered Democrat, was not allowed to vote in the school elections on Tuesday.

Guzzy, on the voting books since May, is an 18-month-old dachshund.

"It's really strange. We haven't the faintest idea how this happened. We registered him with the American Kennel Association," said Christina Garrison, his owner.

Guzzy's voter registration card came in the mail a month ago, but the family thought it was a joke.

Guzzy has now been removed from the voting books.

Headliner

No one was injured this morning when a bus carrying eight persons went out of control.

The brakes failed as the bus was going down a freeway exit ramp. The bus careened across four lanes of traffic and into an automatic car wash, where it came to a stop.

The car wash started and the bus rolled out with a wash and wax.

Headliner

Trio Fished From Ocean

Headliner

Three unidentified sailors were plucked from the Atlantic Ocean by a Norwegian freighter after their 30-foot sailboat sank 200 yards off the coast.

They were tossed about in their tiny orange life raft for four days in chilling, stormy seas. The three were nearly out of food and water and had drifted out of the shipping lanes when rescued.

Headliner

Headliner

Fisherfolk Set For Opening

Headliner

Spilled Trash Litters Roads

Headliner

And Who's Been Eating My Chili?

Headliner

Fish and Wildlife Department officials estimate as many as 750,000 anglers will be out trying their luck Saturday when the general fishing season opens in most of the state.

Most coastal streams will remain closed until May 22. The season will close again Oct. 31.

Headliner

Too much of Spring Valley's trash is ending up on the roadside. This is a growing problem along roads used by Spring Valley residents to haul trash to the sanitary landfill.

Roads are littered when trash falls from cars and trucks going to the garbage dump.

Police will issue citations to motorists for spilling trash from vehicles. The fine is $100 or six months in jail.

Headliner

"Goldilocks and the Three Bears" is supposed to be a fairy tale, but the Vans may think differently after what happened to their cabin in the woods.

The cabin was broken into last week by someone who ate ten packages of chili, popcorn, crackers, and bread.

Evidence indicated that the thief was a messy eater.

It looks as if at least one of the three bears has returned.

Headliner

Headliner

In the News

Purpose   Reading for details in picture captions.

Number of players   3

Materials   In the News game board
             In the News pictures
             In the News captions
             Single die or spinner

Rules   1   Each player positions himself by one of the three
            playing sides of the game board. He draws four In
            the News pictures, placing one on each picture
            space.
        2   The captions are randomly placed on the Hot Line
            (the six numbered spaces), two captions on each
            space.
        3   Each player in turn rolls the die or spins. He draws
            the captions from the Hot Line number that is indi-
            cated on the die or spinner.
        4   The player tries to match the captions to his pictures.
            Any captions that cannot be matched are returned
            to the same Hot Line number.
        5   When a Hot Line number runs out of captions, the
            player who rolls or spins that number loses a turn.
        6   If a player makes an incorrect match, he loses his
            next turn. The player who discovers the incorrect
            match may take an extra turn.
        7   The first player to match each of his pictures to a
            caption is the winner.

| Skateboarders are adding daring new challenges to an already dangerous sport. ITN | Like the straw that broke the camel's back, one too many bags of garbage caused the upending of this garbage truck. ITN | It's art time in the kindergarten class at North Albany Grade School. Clean-up time follows. ITN |
| A row of stop signs decorated the school parking lot when teachers came to work. Where did the stop signs come from? That is a good question. ITN | Ele celebrated his tenth birthday with a cake. He snatched one bite before stepping on the 25-pound cake. ITN | A climber rests after scaling this rugged pinnacle. Climbing mountains has become a popular weekend sport. ITN |

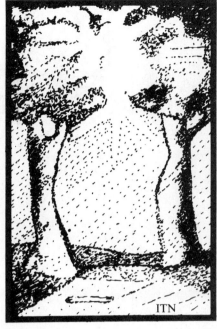

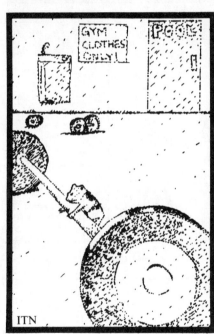

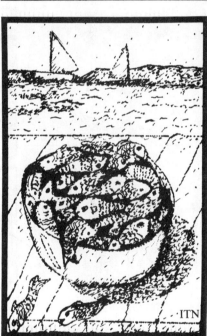

No one was injured when the right front wheel flew off the lead car during yesterday's race. Speeds reached 150 m.p.h.

ITN

Between rain showers, a bright sun managed to squeeze its rays between these two trees.

ITN

Camels, who are not very bright, sometimes seem to think that cars passing through the Wildlife Area are other camels. This camel may have fallen in love with the mini van that it followed through the refuge for over an hour.

ITN

Even frogs must have rigorous training to become winners. Conditioning and diet are important factors for jumpers.

ITN

Three-year-old Mitzi, a beagle, exchanges looks with Sinbad, a passing poodle. While confined to the car, Mitzi's expression seemed to say, "Psst. Open the door."

ITN

Going fishing? You may be hoping to have a catch like this on Opening Day. Saturday is the first day of the season.

ITN

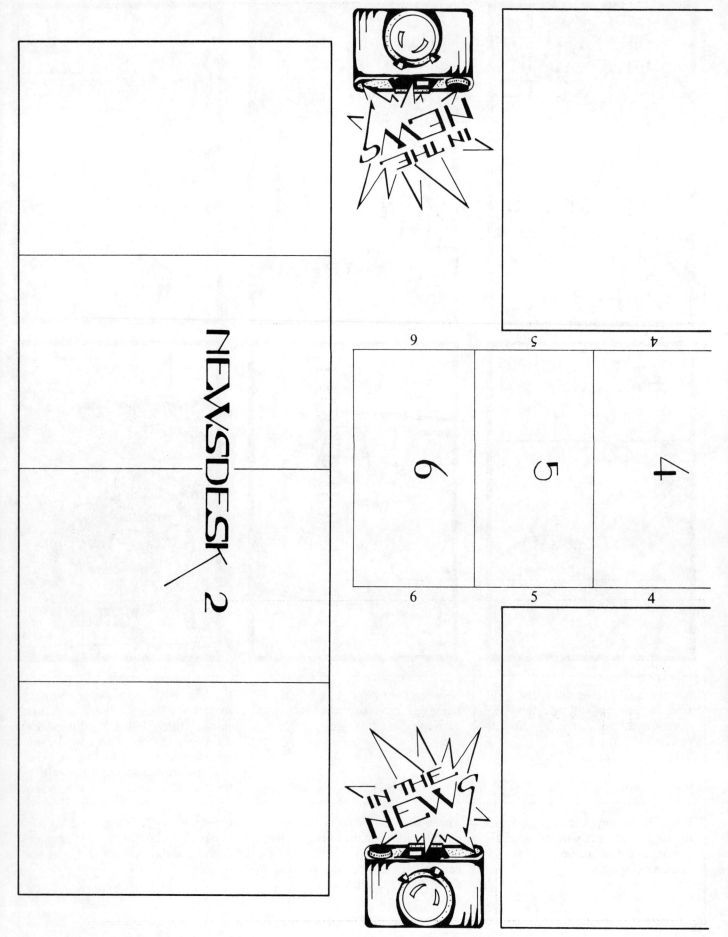

NEWSDESK 2

4
5
6

4
5
6

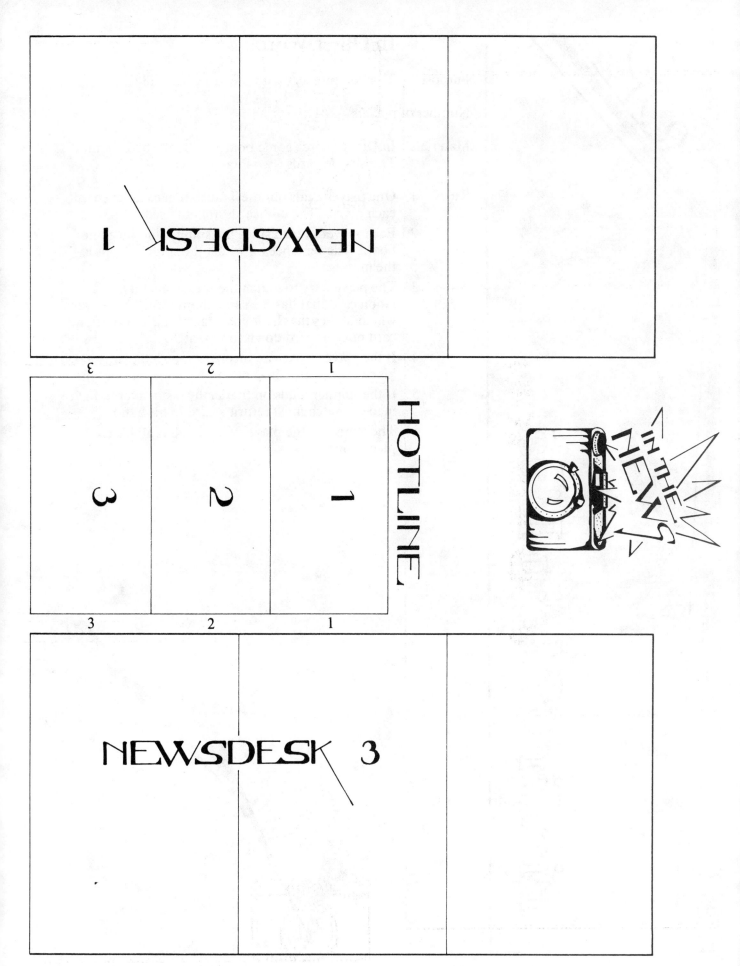

NEWSDESK 1

HOTLINE

1	2	3

NEWSDESK 3

IN THE NEWS

29

3

Finding Main Idea

In Other Words

Purpose   To find sentences with the same main idea.

Number of players   2–4

Materials   In Other Words game board with attached spinner
Translation cards (two identical sets)

Rules   1   One player deals out the Translation cards evenly to
each player. The odd cards are not used.

2   Each player in turn spins the spinner on the game
board. The sentence on which the spinner stops is
the message.

3   The players try to match the message with a Translation card that has the same main idea. The player
who first sees that he holds a matching Translation
card puts his card down for a match.

4   If the player makes an incorrect match, he must take
his card back and drop out of the game for one spin.

5   If the spinner lands on Static, the last player to have
made a match must return a card to his hand.

6   The winner is the player who first has all his cards
placed down.

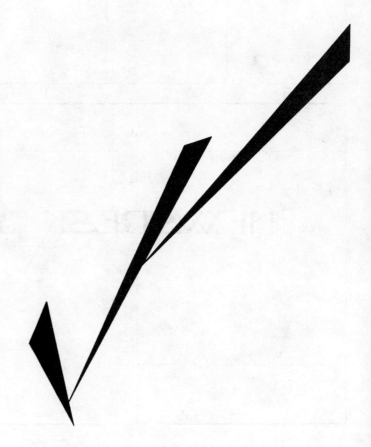

There are two kinds of camels.	Alice fell asleep and had a nightmare.	The family packed their car for a long trip.
translation	**translation**	**translation**
in other words	in other words	in other words
Reaching out into the lake was a wooden dock.	Two hikers were climbing the mountain.	People waited impatiently, looking down the street.
translation	**translation**	**translation**
in other words	in other words	in other words
Squirrels hurried here and there through the forest.	The adventurer returned from a long trip.	The small elf was like nothing I had ever seen before.
translation	**translation**	**translation**
in other words	in other words	in other words
Wilbur often asked his mother questions.		
translation		
in other words		

in other words

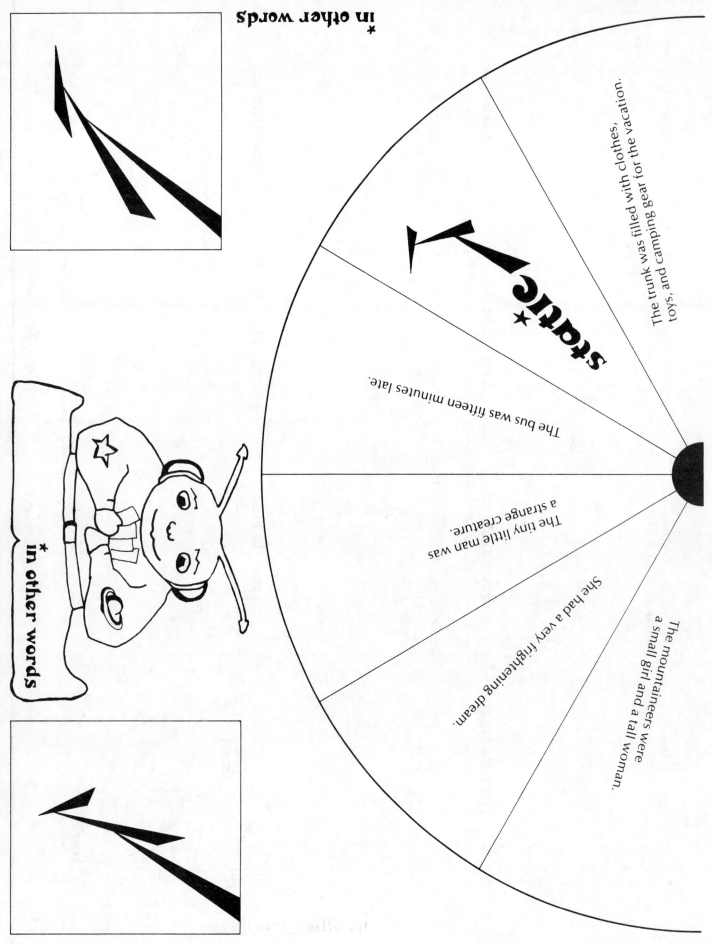

The spinning board content:

- in other words
- static
- The trunk was filled with clothes, toys, and camping gear for the vacation.
- The bus was fifteen minutes late.
- The tiny little man was a strange creature.
- She had a very frightening dream.
- The mountaineers were a small girl and a tall woman.
- in other words

32   To complete the board, push a brad through the center

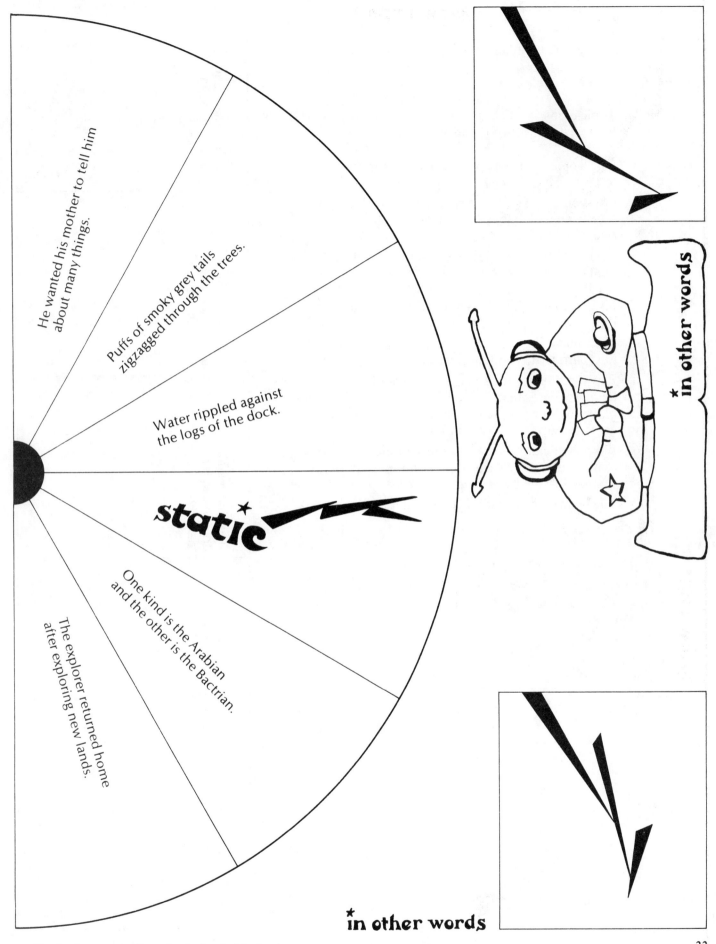

He wanted his mother to tell him about many things.

Puffs of smoky grey tails zigzagged through the trees.

Water rippled against the logs of the dock.

static

One kind is the Arabian and the other is the Bactrian.

The explorer returned home after exploring new lands.

*in other words

*in other words

and hook a large paper clip under the head of the brad.

Focus

Purpose   To find the main idea, or topic, of sentence groups.

Number of players   2 or 4

Materials   Topic cards
Sentence cards (two identical sets)

Rules
1. One Topic card and five Sentence cards are dealt out to each player.
2. The remaining sentence cards are placed in a pile facedown with one turned faceup for the discard pile.
3. Each player in turn draws a Sentence card. If the Sentence card matches (pertains to the main idea of) his Topic card, he keeps it and discards another of his cards faceup. If the sentence card is not a match, the player discards it faceup.
4. Each player in turn may draw the top discard or the next card in the Sentence card pile.
5. Play continues until a player has a book of five Sentence cards that match his Topic card. When a player has a book, he calls out "Focus" and lays his cards faceup for the other players to check.
6. If a player calls "Focus" but has an incorrect book (with one or more cards that do not pertain to his Topic card), he loses the game.
7. The winner is the first player who has a correct book.

TOPIC FOCUS	TOPIC FOCUS	TOPIC FOCUS	TOPIC FOCUS
The wild horses returned.	There were bears in the dark woods.	It was the day of the big game.	The island was very interesting.

The old mare and stallion stood in the middle.	SENTENCE FOCUS
Each horse had a little pile of cornmeal.	SENTENCE FOCUS
The colt began to drink water eagerly.	SENTENCE FOCUS
The wind blew through their manes.	SENTENCE FOCUS
Each whinnied once.	SENTENCE FOCUS

34

Bears are hungry this time of year.

FOCUS SENTENCE

The score was tied.

FOCUS SENTENCE

The beach was quite sandy.

FOCUS SENTENCE

There were paw prints in the open field.

FOCUS SENTENCE

The last batter was up to bat.

FOCUS SENTENCE

The ocean had tossed up unusual shells.

FOCUS SENTENCE

The tree's bark was torn where claws had been sharpened.

FOCUS SENTENCE

The runner slid into first base.

FOCUS SENTENCE

Pieces of driftwood littered the beach.

FOCUS SENTENCE

It was scary in the dark woods.

FOCUS SENTENCE

The umpire called "Strike two."

FOCUS SENTENCE

The wreckage of a ship poked up through the sand.

FOCUS SENTENCE

A bear can run faster than a man.

FOCUS SENTENCE

Then the other team was up to bat.

FOCUS SENTENCE

Pirate treasure was buried somewhere in the sand.

FOCUS SENTENCE

Duplicate two sets of Sentence cards.

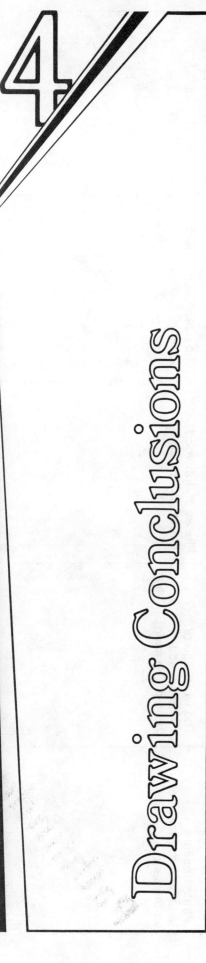

Drawing Conclusions

Pathfinder

Purpose   To draw conclusions from a story that all the players have read.

Number of players   2–4

Materials   Pathfinder game board
Adventure cards
Single die or spinner
Marker for each player

Rules   1   Each player in turn rolls the die or spins and moves his marker the number of spaces shown.

       2   To stay where he lands, the player must satisfactorily answer the question.

       3   If the player gives an unsatisfactory answer, he must go back to his previous space.

       4   If a player lands on an Adventure space, he must draw a card and follow the directions. The player moves ahead two spaces if he responds correctly and back two spaces if he responds incorrectly. If the card refers to the Rapids, the Pine Forest, or the Berry Patch, the player moves to the appropriate space.

       5   The first player to reach the Tree House is the winner.

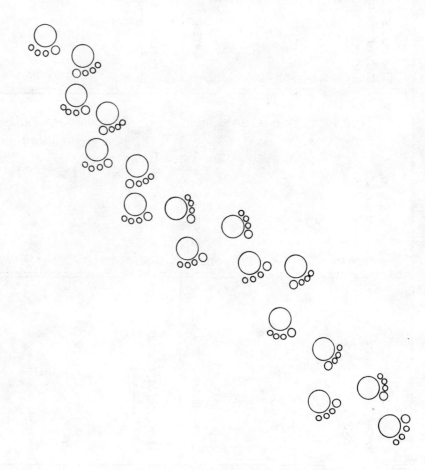

How would the story have
differed if the setting
were in a foreign country?

Pathfinder Adventure

How would the story have
differed if the setting
were in a desert?

Pathfinder Adventure

Tell a different ending
for the story.

Pathfinder Adventure

What kind of hobbies
do you think the main
character would enjoy?

Pathfinder Adventure

Did the characters treat
one another fairly?
Why or why not?

Pathfinder Adventure

Caught in the Rapids.
Lose a turn.

Pathfinder Adventure

Lost in the Pine Forest.
Lose a turn.

Pathfinder Adventure

Discover Berry Patch.
Take another turn.

Pathfinder Adventure

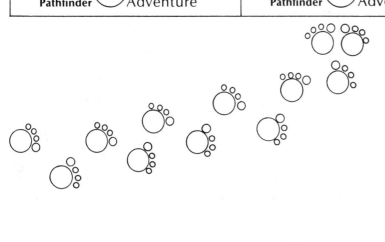

Pathfinder

Pathfinder

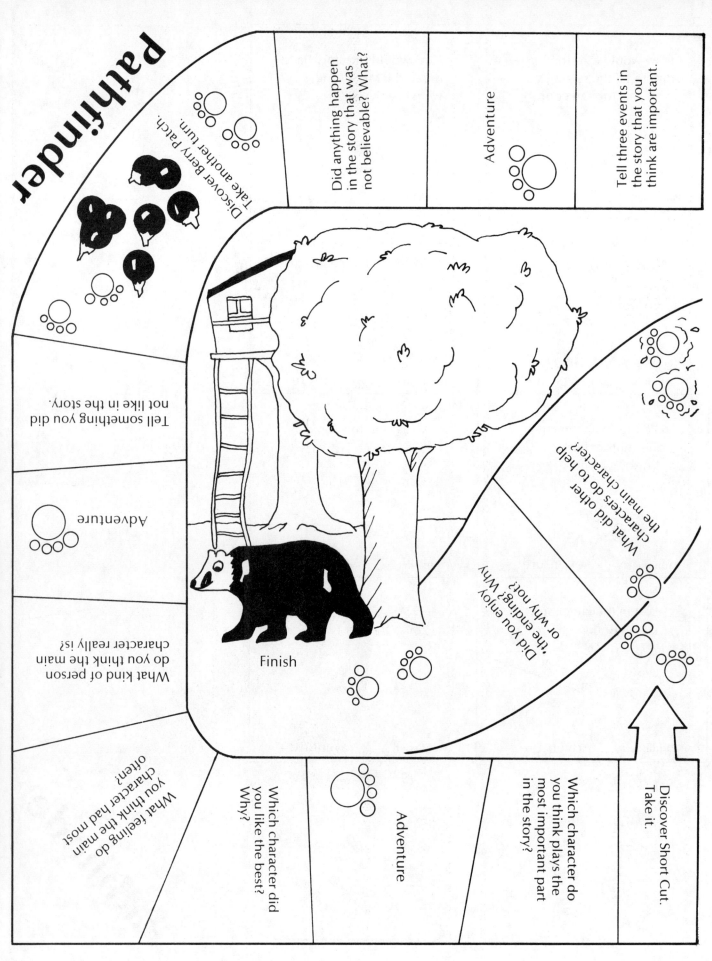

Discover berry patch.
Take another turn.

Did anything happen
in the story that was
not believable? What?

Adventure

Tell three events in
the story that you
think are important.

Tell something you did
not like in the story.

Adventure

What kind of person
do you think the main
character really is?

What did other
characters do to help
the main character?

Did you enjoy
the ending? Why
or why not?

Finish

What feeling do
you think the main
character had most
often?

Which character did
you like the best?
Why?

Adventure

Which character do
you think plays the
most important part
in the story?

Discover Short Cut.
Take it.

38

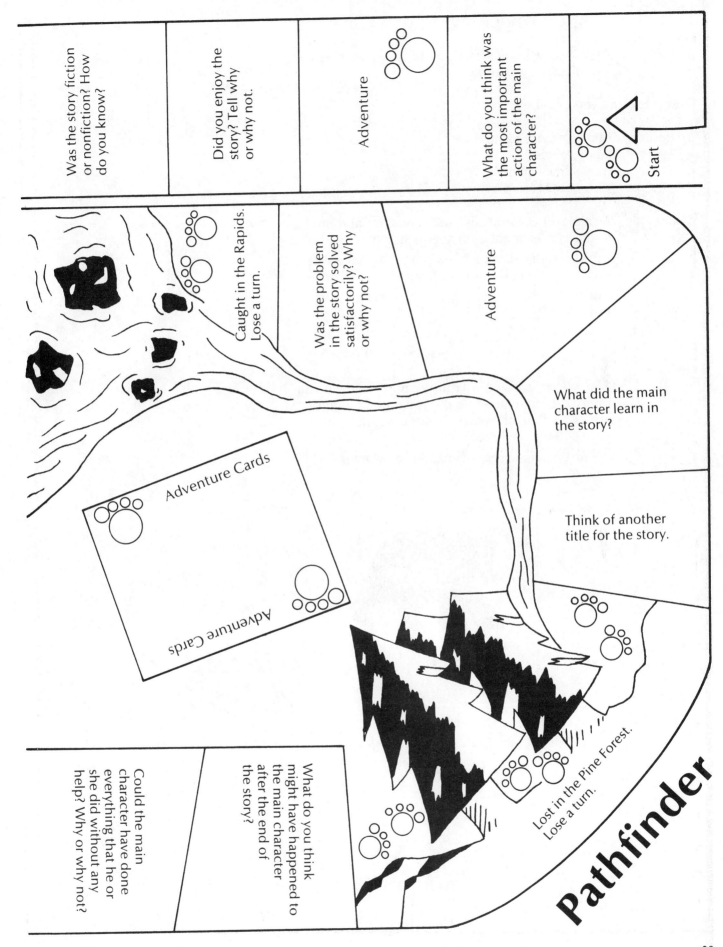

Was the story fiction or nonfiction? How do you know?

Did you enjoy the story? Tell why or why not.

Adventure

What do you think was the most important action of the main character?

Start

Caught in the Rapids. Lose a turn.

Was the problem in the story solved satisfactorily? Why or why not?

Adventure

What did the main character learn in the story?

Adventure Cards

Adventure Cards

Think of another title for the story.

Lost in the Pine Forest. Lose a turn.

What do you think might have happened to the main character after the end of the story?

Could the main character have done everything that he or she did without any help? Why or why not?

Pathfinder

Taking Advice

Purpose   To draw conclusions by associating words of advice with pictured situations.

Number of players   2–4

Materials   Taking Advice game board
Advice cards
Single die or spinner
Marker for each player

Rules 1   Each player in turn rolls the die or spins and moves his marker the number of spaces shown.

2   If the player lands on a blank space, he has a free turn.

3   If the player lands on a picture, he loses his next turn.

4   If the player lands on a space occupied by another player, the first player on the space must return to Start.

5   If the player lands on a Trouble space, he draws an Advice card and moves to the corresponding picture. More than one player may occupy a picture space at the same time.

6   The first player to reach Finish is the winner.

Taking Advice

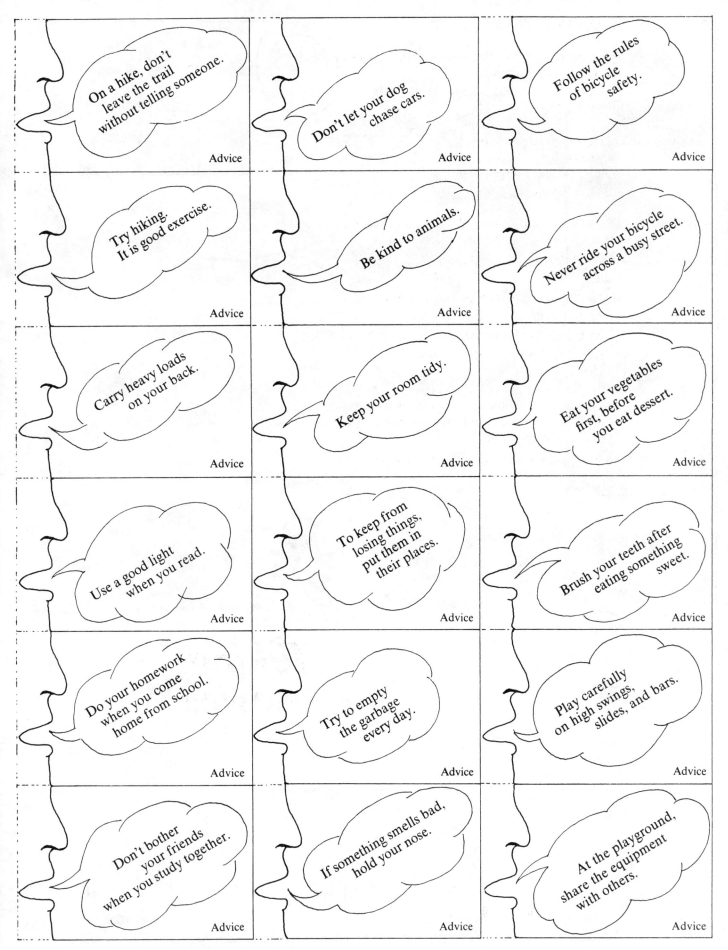

41

Trouble

Trouble

Taking Advice

Trouble

Finish

Trouble

Start

Trouble

42

Taking Advice

Advice
Cards

Trouble

Trouble

Trouble

Trouble

Trouble

Trouble

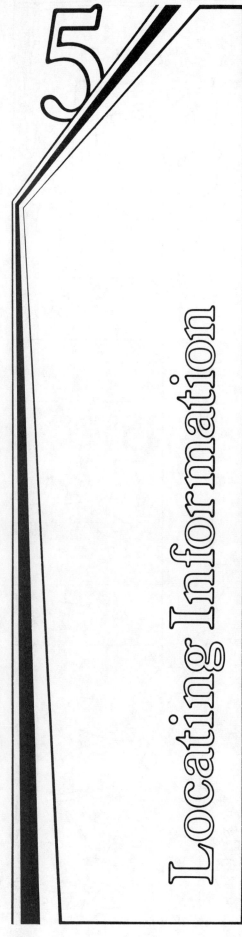

5

Locating Information

Step Along

Purpose To use charts in locating information.

Number of players 2–4

Materials Step Along game board
Here cards and There cards
Step Along chart
Single die or spinner
Marker for each player

Rules

1 The Here and There cards are placed facedown in two piles. Each player in turn draws a card from each pile. He then refers to the chart to tell how many steps there are between the two locations in the school.

2 If the player responds correctly, he may roll the die or spin and move the number of spaces shown. He starts at IN and moves clockwise around the outer hallway.

3 If the player answers incorrectly, he must stay in the same position for that turn.

4 When a player lands on an intersection space (marked DETOUR), he must take the side hallway. If he lands on the intersection space as he leaves the hallway, the player must turn around and again move down the hallway.

5 If a player lands on a space in front of a classroom door, he may take another turn.

6 When a player's turn is completed, he buries his cards in the appropriate piles.

7 The first player to reach OUT is the winner.

Step Along

	Cafeteria	Gym	Health Room	Library	Music Room	Principal	First Grade	Second Grade	Third Grade	Fourth Grade	Fifth Grade	Sixth Grade
Cafeteria	0	60	80	20	100	45	65	85	105	120	105	110
Gym	60	0	135	75	135	100	120	140	130	115	80	55
Health Room	80	135	0	65	25	40	20	10	30	45	80	105
Library	20	75	65	0	85	30	50	70	90	105	90	115
Music Room	100	135	25	85	0	60	40	20	10	25	60	85
Principal	45	100	40	30	60	0	25	45	65	80	75	100
First Grade	65	120	20	50	40	25	0	25	45	60	95	120
Second Grade	85	140	10	70	20	45	25	0	25	40	75	100
Third Grade	105	130	30	90	10	65	45	25	0	20	55	80
Fourth Grade	120	115	45	105	25	80	60	40	20	0	40	65
Fifth Grade	105	80	80	90	60	75	95	75	55	40	0	30
Sixth Grade	110	55	105	115	85	100	120	100	80	65	30	0

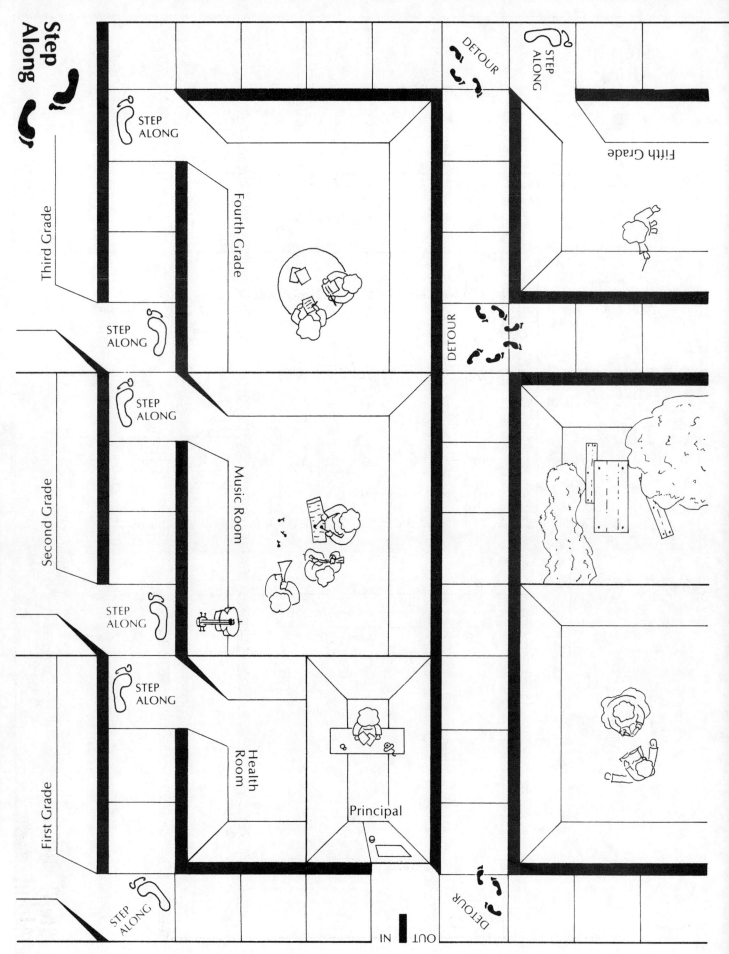

Step Along

Third Grade

Fourth Grade

STEP ALONG

STEP ALONG

STEP ALONG

Second Grade

Music Room

STEP ALONG

STEP ALONG

First Grade

Health Room

Principal

STEP ALONG

OUT IN

DETOUR

DETOUR

DETOUR

STEP ALONG

Fifth Grade

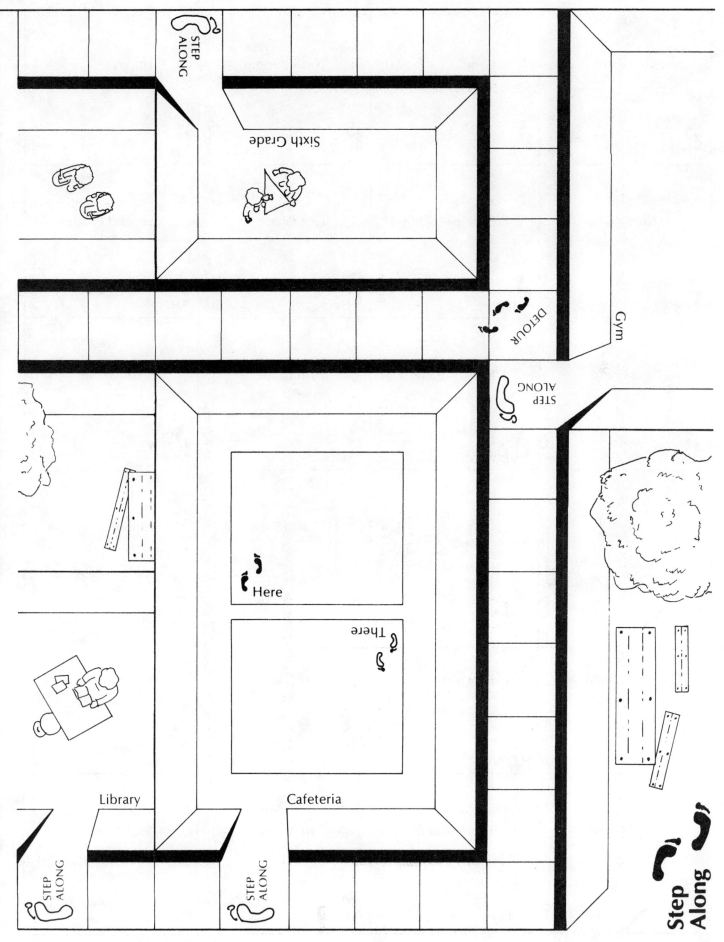

Cafeteria	Gym	Health Room	Library
Here Step Along	Here Step Along	Here Step Along	Here Step Along
Music Room	Principal's Office	First Grade	Second Grade
Here Step Along	Here Step Along	Here Step Along	Here Step Along
Third Grade	Fourth Grade	Fifth Grade	Sixth Grade
Here Step Along	Here Step Along	Here Step Along	Here Step Along
Cafeteria	Gym	Health Room	Library
There Step Along	There Step Along	There Step Along	There Step Along
Music Room	Principal's Office	First Grade	Second Grade
There Step Along	There Step Along	There Step Along	There Step Along
Third Grade	Fourth Grade	Fifth Grade	Sixth Grade
There Step Along	There Step Along	There Step Along	There Step Along

Grapho

Purpose   To use bar graphs in locating information.

Number of players   2–4

Materials   Grapho game board
              Single die or spinner
              Marker for each player

Rules   1   Each player in turn rolls the die or spins and moves
            his marker the number of spaces shown.

        2   The player notes the number on which he lands.
            That number represents the age of some people in
            "Our Town, USA." The player reads the graph and
            states the number of people that are that age.

        3   To stay where he lands, the player must correctly
            read the bar graph.

        4   If the player responds incorrectly, he must return to
            his previous position.

        5   If a player lands on a Grapho space, he moves his
            marker either ahead or back to the other Grapho
            space with the same face.

        6   The first player to reach Finish is the winner.

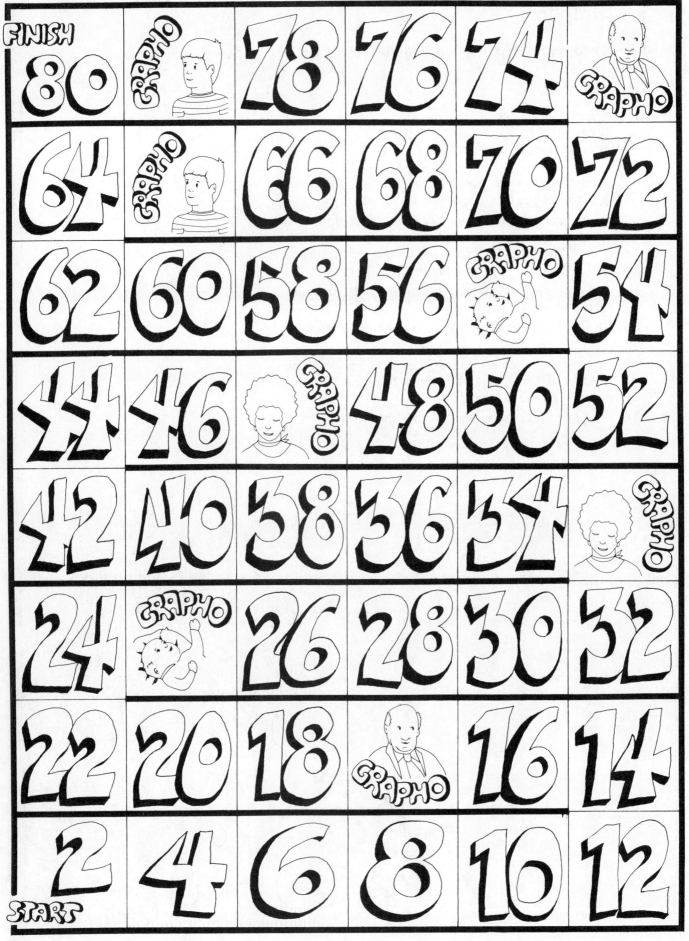

Population of Our Town, USA

Search

Purpose   To locate information through a table of contents.

Number of players   2–4

Materials   Search game board
             Search cards
             Table of Contents
             Single die or spinner
             Marker for each player

Rules   1   Each player in turn rolls the die or spins and moves
              his marker the number of spaces shown.
         2   The player answers the question on which he lands
              by using the Table of Contents.
         3   If a player cannot answer correctly, he must return
              his marker to its previous position.
         4   If a player lands on a Search space, he draws a
              Search card and follows the directions.
         5   The first player to reach Finish is the winner.

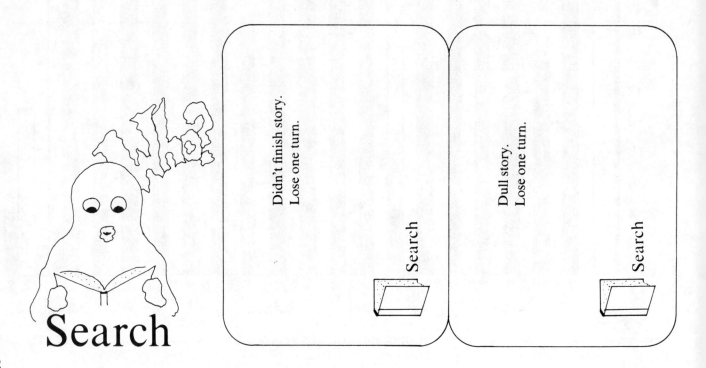

Table of Contents

Search

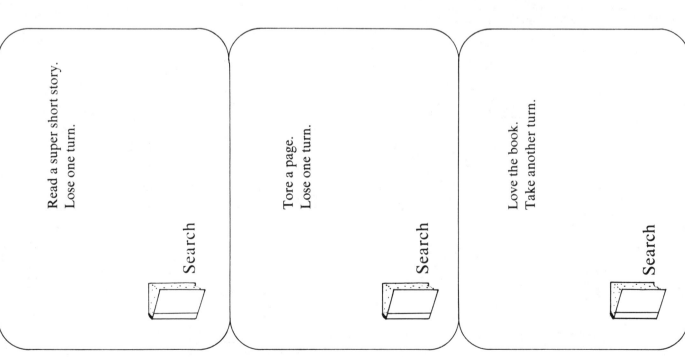

Read a super short story.
Lose one turn.

Search

Tore a page.
Lose one turn.

Search

Love the book.
Take another turn.

Search

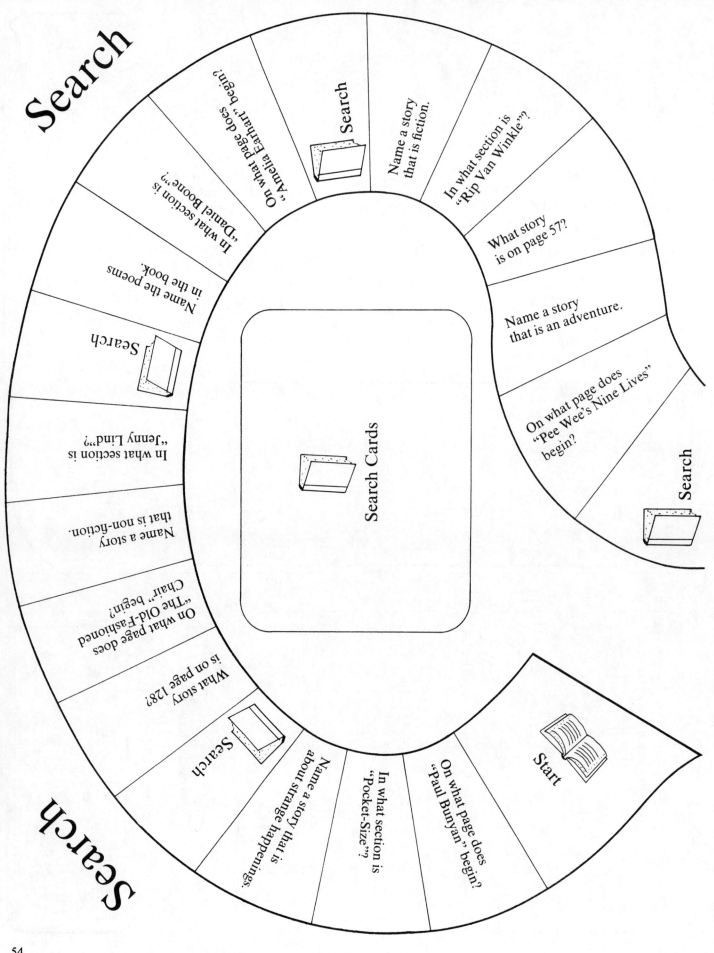

Search

Search

Search

Name a story
that is fiction.

In what section is
"Rip Van Winkle"?

What story
is on page 57?

Name a story
that is an adventure.

On what page does
"Pee Wee's Nine Lives"
begin?

Search

On what page does
"Amelia Earhart" begin?

In what section is
"Daniel Boone"?

Name the poems
in the book.

Search

In what section is
"Jenny Lind"?

Name a story
that is non-fiction.

On what page does
"The Old-Fashioned
Chair" begin?

What story
is on page 128?

Search

Search Cards

Name a story that is
about strange
happenings.

In what section is
"Pocket-Size"?

On what page does
"Paul Bunyan" begin?

Start

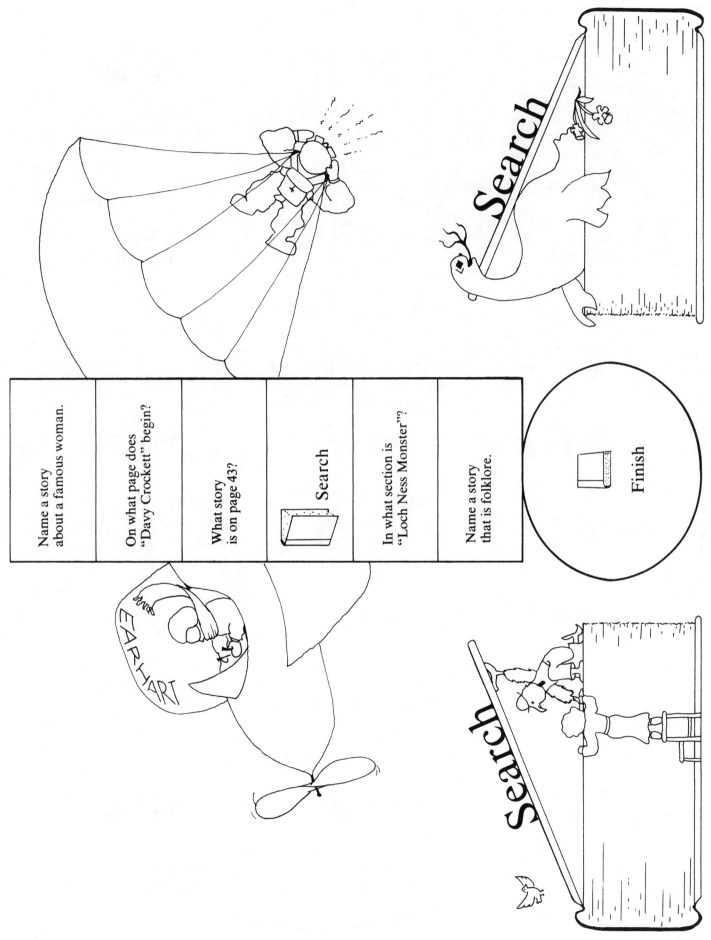

Name a story
about a famous woman.

On what page does
"Davy Crockett" begin?

What story
is on page 43?

Search

In what section is
"Loch Ness Monster"?

Name a story
that is folklore.

Finish

Search

Search

Information Please

Purpose   To use the encyclopedia for locating information.

Number of players   2–4

Materials   Information Please game board
             Information Please cards
             Bookworm cards
             Single die or spinner
             Marker for each player

Rules   1   Each player in turn draws an Information Please card and states in which encyclopedia volume the information can be found.

2   If the player responds correctly, he rolls the die or spins and moves the number of spaces shown.

3   If the player responds incorrectly, he loses that turn.

4   Play continues across the board and back. The top half of the encyclopedias counts one space each and the bottom half of the set counts one space each.

5   If a player lands on a space also occupied by a Bookworm, he draws a Bookworm card and follows the directions.

6   The first player to reach Finish is the winner.

INFORMATION PLEASE

Want to know more about bananas. Move to Volume B, top half.

Bookworm

Information Please

Find out about the Mayan Indians. Move to Volume M, top half.

Bookworm

Information Please

Write a report on unicorns. Move to Volume U, top half.

Bookworm

Information Please

First to complete a report on dogs. Take another turn.

Bookworm

Information Please

INFORMATION PLEASE — John James Audubon

INFORMATION PLEASE — Mary Ritter Beard

INFORMATION PLEASE — Carbon

INFORMATION PLEASE — Eclipse

INFORMATION PLEASE — Heredity

INFORMATION PLEASE — Atlantic Ocean

INFORMATION PLEASE — Batik

INFORMATION PLEASE — Juan Cabrillo

INFORMATION PLEASE — Babe Didrikson

INFORMATION PLEASE — Gold

More Information Please cards on page 60.

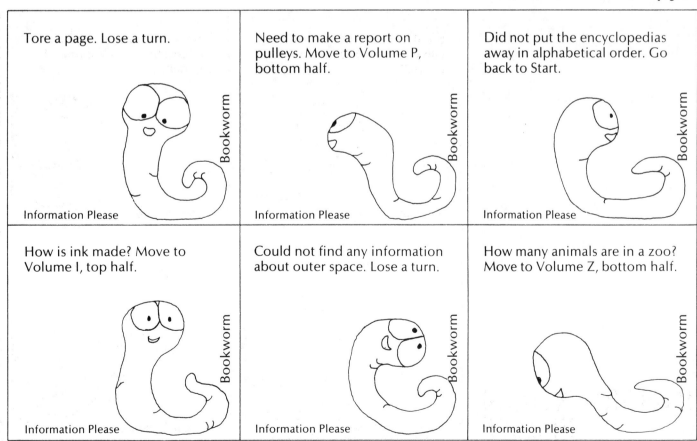

Tore a page. Lose a turn.
Bookworm
Information Please

Need to make a report on pulleys. Move to Volume P, bottom half.
Bookworm
Information Please

Did not put the encyclopedias away in alphabetical order. Go back to Start.
Bookworm
Information Please

How is ink made? Move to Volume I, top half.
Bookworm
Information Please

Could not find any information about outer space. Lose a turn.
Bookworm
Information Please

How many animals are in a zoo? Move to Volume Z, bottom half.
Bookworm
Information Please

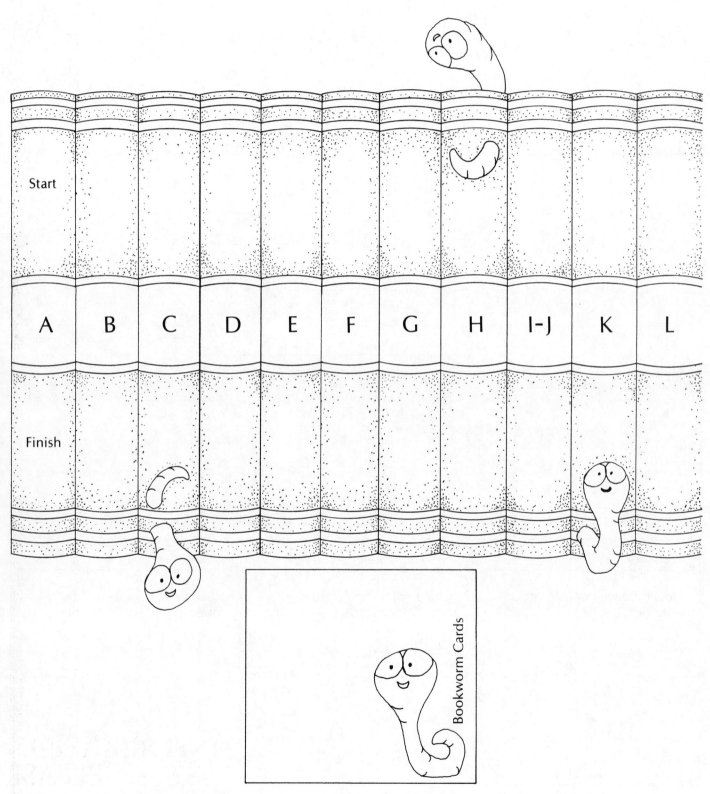

Start

A   B   C   D   E   F   G   H   I-J   K   L

Finish

Bookworm Cards

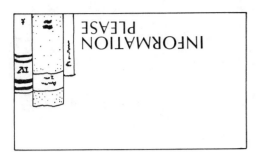

INFORMATION
PLEASE

Martin Luther King	Jelly fish	Incubation
INFORMATION PLEASE	INFORMATION PLEASE	INFORMATION PLEASE
Ottawa	Nickel	Navajo
INFORMATION PLEASE	INFORMATION PLEASE	INFORMATION PLEASE
Sacajawea	Quail	Porcupine
INFORMATION PLEASE	INFORMATION PLEASE	INFORMATION PLEASE
Venezuela	Ukulele	Trout
INFORMATION PLEASE	INFORMATION PLEASE	INFORMATION PLEASE
Zeppelin	Xylophone	Earl Warren
INFORMATION PLEASE	INFORMATION PLEASE	INFORMATION PLEASE

Lettuce	Jesse Owens	Schooner
INFORMATION PLEASE	INFORMATION PLEASE	INFORMATION PLEASE
Warbler		
INFORMATION PLEASE		

Book Nook

Purpose   To use the library card catalog for locating information.

Number of players   2–4

Materials   Book Nook gameboard for each player
Set of Book Nook cards for each player

Rules   1   Each player is given a Book Nook game board, representing a card catalog.

2   The sets of cards are shuffled together and placed in a pile facedown.

3   Each player in turn draws a card and places it faceup on the card file drawer in which it would be located.

4   If a player draws a card that belongs on a drawer where he has already placed a card, he must return the card to the bottom of the pile and lose that turn.

5   The first player to correctly match a card to every drawer in his card catalog is the winner.

E Br. Airplanes Brown, Alice BOOK NOOK A-Z	F Rey. Dollars For Fun Reyhner, Margaret BOOK NOOK A-Z	793 Co. Jokes for Laughs Cook, Curt BOOK NOOK A-Z
E Jo. Big Noise Johnson, Amy BOOK NOOK A-Z	398.2 Folklore W. Workinger, Howard Tales of School BOOK NOOK A-Z	F Hu. Missy Hutson, Albert BOOK NOOK A-Z
F Car. Carlson, Betty The Empty Box BOOK NOOK A-Z	E Ga. Gates, June All Kinds of Fences BOOK NOOK A-Z	920 Th. Kennedy—35th President Thurston, Lynn BOOK NOOK A-Z
598.1 Crocodiles M. Meredith, Opal Crocodiles and Alligators BOOK NOOK A-Z	E Bar. Hello Friends Barnes, Ruby BOOK NOOK A-Z	612 La. Landon, George The Human Body BOOK NOOK A-Z
BOOK NOOK A-Z	E Be. In To Dinner Beatty, Horace BOOK NOOK A-Z	538.07 Magnetism Ga. Garns, Naomi Experimenting with Magnets BOOK NOOK A-Z

F Fr. Mystery on Chintimini Hill Fryk, Cindy BOOK NOOK A-Z	385　　　　　　Railroads Pe. Peters, Ted Development of Railroads BOOK NOOK A-Z	F Van. Van Leuven, Enid Fun! Fun! Fun! BOOK NOOK A-Z
398.8　　　Nursery Rhymes Ba. Bacer, Trudy Goosey Tales BOOK NOOK A-Z	F Hu. Runaway Sam Hurst, Grace BOOK NOOK A-Z	E Go. White Crow Gordon, Bill BOOK NOOK A-Z
332　　　　Occupations Br. Brent, Carol A Job for You BOOK NOOK A-Z	921 Sm. Smith, Gregory Indian Legends BOOK NOOK A-Z	F Ta. The Teaser Tabor, Jerry BOOK NOOK A-Z
F Bl. Penny the Penguin Blue, Byrdis BOOK NOOK A-Z	F Re. Tacos For Sale Reist, Kathleen BOOK NOOK A-Z	590　　　　　　Zebras St. Striper, Kay Zebras in Captivity BOOK NOOK A-Z
F Be. Quicksand Beach, Sandy BOOK NOOK A-Z	582　　　　　　Trees Gl. Glebb, Joyce How to Identify Conifers BOOK NOOK A-Z	BOOK NOOK A-Z

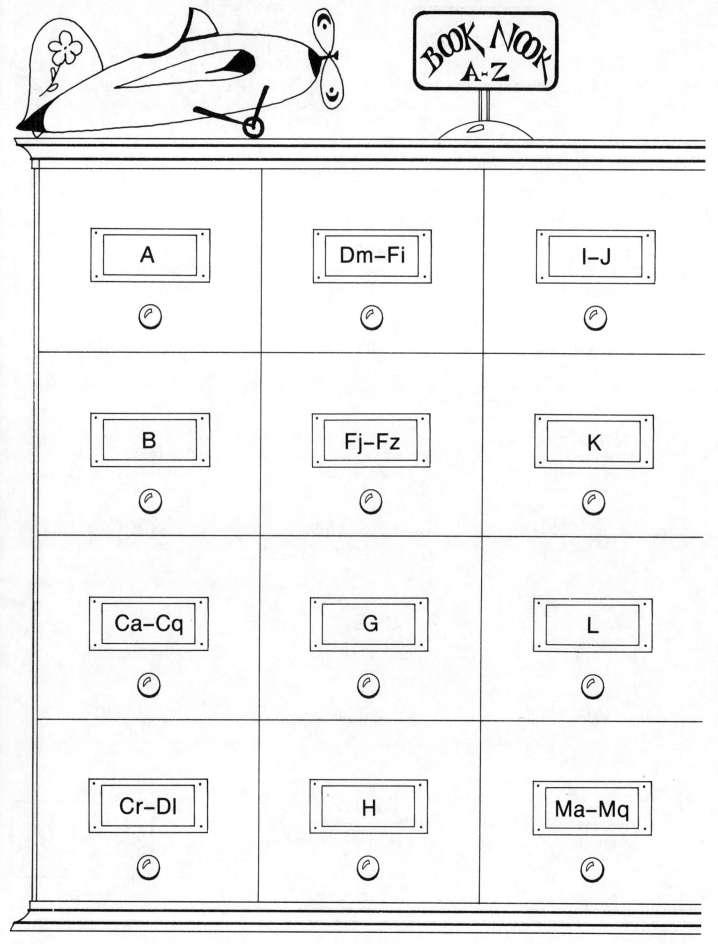

Mr–No	Ra–Rt	Tp–Tz
Np–Nz	Ru–Si	U–V
O	Sj–Sz	W
P–Q	Ta–To	X–Y–Z

Ski Trail

Purpose   To use maps and map legends for locating infor-
           mation.

Number of players   2–4

Materials   Ski Trail game board
            Sitz cards
            Single die or spinner
            Marker for each player

Rules   1   Each player in turn rolls the die or spins and moves
            his marker the number of spaces shown.
        2   If a player lands on a Sitz Mark (a hole in the snow
            created when a skier falls, represented on the board
            by a fallen skier), he draws a Sitz card.
        3   The player reads the directions on the card and
            follows the directions by using the legend, moving to
            the appropriate numbered or lettered space.
        4   The first player to return to the parking lot is the
            winner.

SKI TRAIL

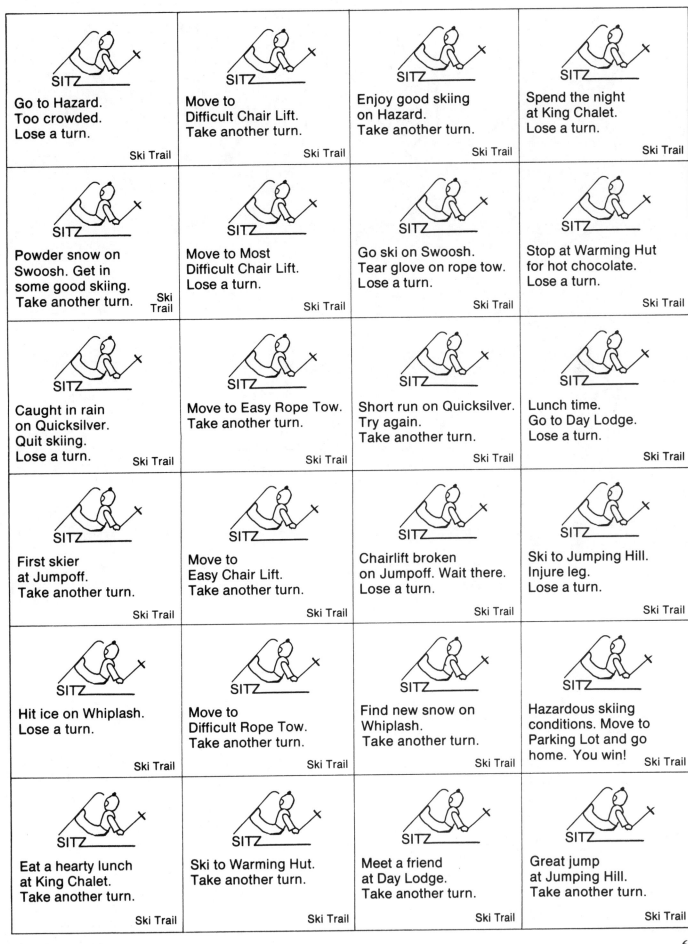

Go to Hazard.
Too crowded.
Lose a turn.

Ski Trail

Move to
Difficult Chair Lift.
Take another turn.

Ski Trail

Enjoy good skiing
on Hazard.
Take another turn.

Ski Trail

Spend the night
at King Chalet.
Lose a turn.

Ski Trail

Powder snow on
Swoosh. Get in
some good skiing.
Take another turn.

Ski
Trail

Move to Most
Difficult Chair Lift.
Lose a turn.

Ski Trail

Go ski on Swoosh.
Tear glove on rope tow.
Lose a turn.

Ski Trail

Stop at Warming Hut
for hot chocolate.
Lose a turn.

Ski Trail

Caught in rain
on Quicksilver.
Quit skiing.
Lose a turn.

Ski Trail

Move to Easy Rope Tow.
Take another turn.

Ski Trail

Short run on Quicksilver.
Try again.
Take another turn.

Ski Trail

Lunch time.
Go to Day Lodge.
Lose a turn.

Ski Trail

First skier
at Jumpoff.
Take another turn.

Ski Trail

Move to
Easy Chair Lift.
Take another turn.

Ski Trail

Chairlift broken
on Jumpoff. Wait there.
Lose a turn.

Ski Trail

Ski to Jumping Hill.
Injure leg.
Lose a turn.

Ski Trail

Hit ice on Whiplash.
Lose a turn.

Ski Trail

Move to
Difficult Rope Tow.
Take another turn.

Ski Trail

Find new snow on
Whiplash.
Take another turn.

Ski Trail

Hazardous skiing
conditions. Move to
Parking Lot and go
home. You win!

Ski Trail

Eat a hearty lunch
at King Chalet.
Take another turn.

Ski Trail

Ski to Warming Hut.
Take another turn.

Ski Trail

Meet a friend
at Day Lodge.
Take another turn.

Ski Trail

Great jump
at Jumping Hill.
Take another turn.

Ski Trail

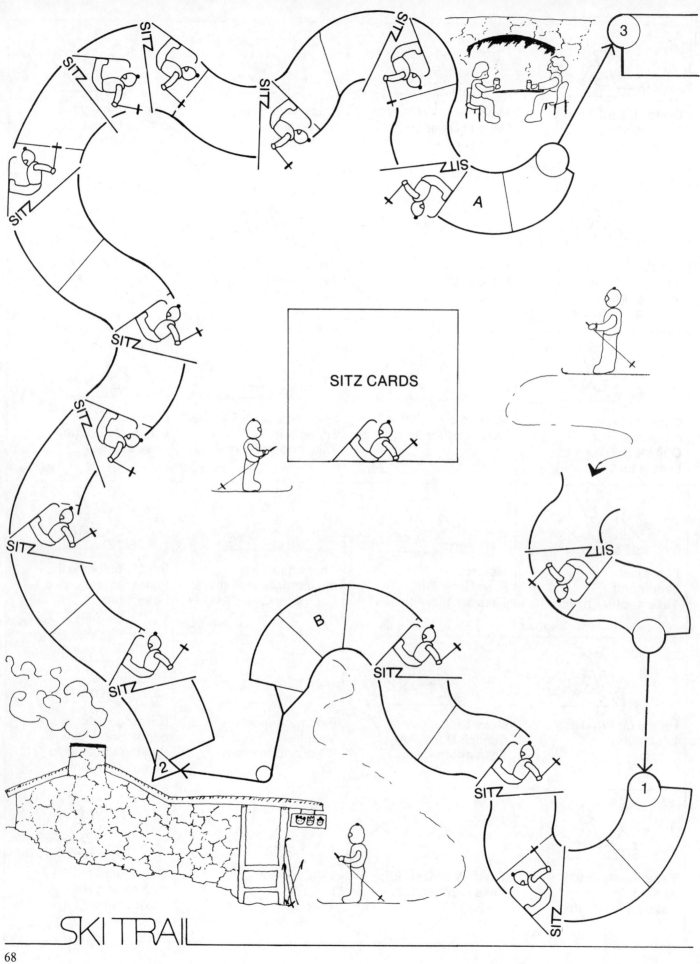

SITZ CARDS

SKI TRAIL

68

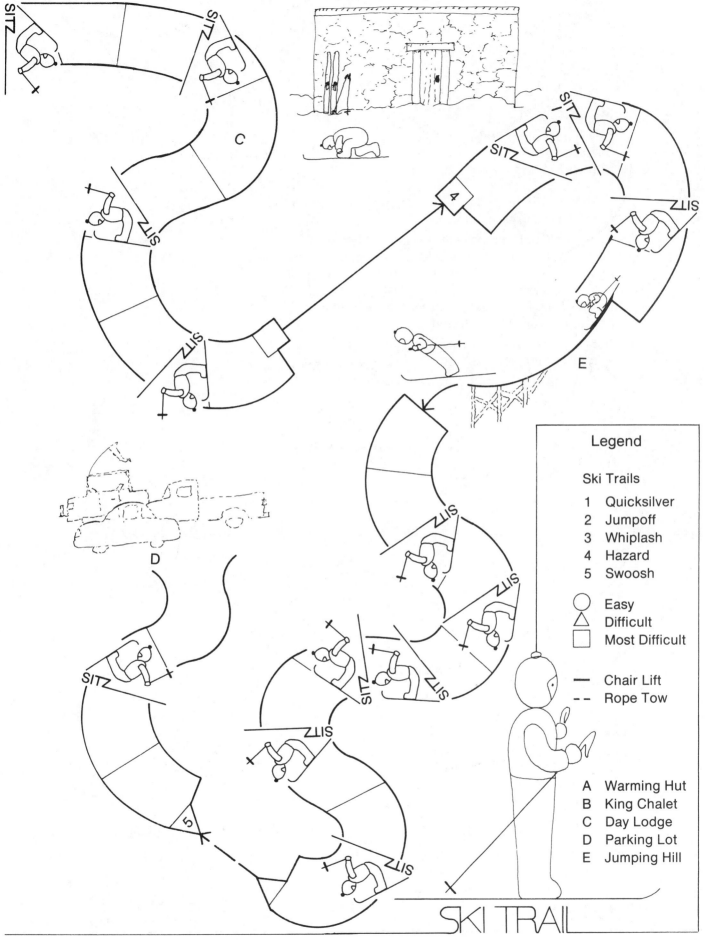

Legend

Ski Trails

1 Quicksilver
2 Jumpoff
3 Whiplash
4 Hazard
5 Swoosh

○ Easy
△ Difficult
☐ Most Difficult

— Chair Lift
-- Rope Tow

A Warming Hut
B King Chalet
C Day Lodge
D Parking Lot
E Jumping Hill

SKI TRAIL

Wanted

Purpose   To locate information using newspaper indexes.

Number of players   2–4

Materials   Wanted game board
Newspaper index and Classified index
Single die or spinner
Marker for each player

Rules   1   Each player in turn rolls the die or spins and moves
the number of spaces shown.
2   To stay where he lands, a player must follow the
directions on that space, using the Newspaper index
to find the correct section of the paper. If the correct
section is Classified, he must then use the Classified
index to identify the key number that tells where
appropriate ads can be found.
3   If a player answers incorrectly, he must move back 7
spaces, but not beyond Start.
4   The first player to reach Finish is the winner.

dit.
stude
s for old
Experience
and of work for
ed vocalist and le
rage sale Sunday at
rigerator **WANTED** so
ousehold. Call evenings af
dle puppies for sale to good

Classified Index

Newspaper Index

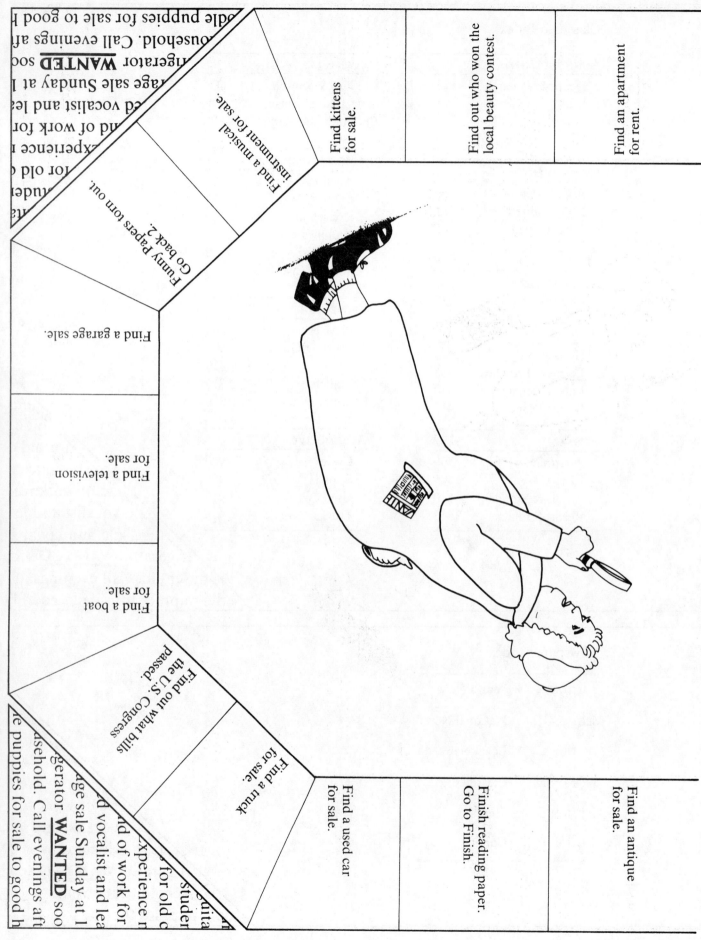

Find kittens for sale.

Find out who won the local beauty contest.

Find an apartment for rent.

Find a musical instrument for sale.

Funny papers torn out. Go back 2.

Find a garage sale.

Find a television for sale.

Find a boat for sale.

Find out what bills the U.S. Congress passed.

Find a truck for sale.

Find a used car for sale.

Finish reading paper. Go to Finish.

Find an antique for sale.

72

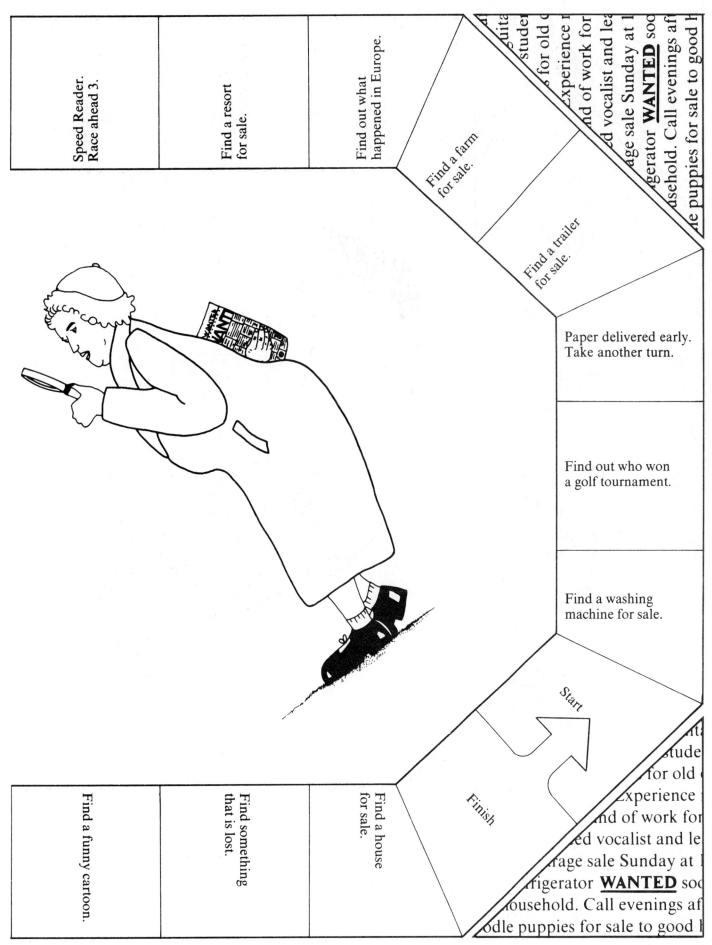

Speed Reader.
Race ahead 3.

Find a resort
for sale.

Find out what
happened in Europe.

Find a farm
for sale.

Find a trailer
for sale.

Paper delivered early.
Take another turn.

Find out who won
a golf tournament.

Find a washing
machine for sale.

Start

Finish

Find a house
for sale.

Find something
that is lost.

Find a funny cartoon.

WANTED

6

Distinguishing Fact from Opinion

Cat and Mouse

Purpose   To distinguish fact from opinion in a series of statements.

Number of players   2–4

Materials   Cat and Mouse game board
Single die or spinner
Marker for each player

Rules
1   Each player in turn rolls the die or spins and moves the number of spaces shown.
2   To stay where he lands, the player must correctly answer whether the statement on that space is fact or opinion.
3   If the player answers incorrectly, he must move ahead two spaces.
4   The first player to reach the cat is the loser. The winner is the player closest to Start when another player lands on the cat.

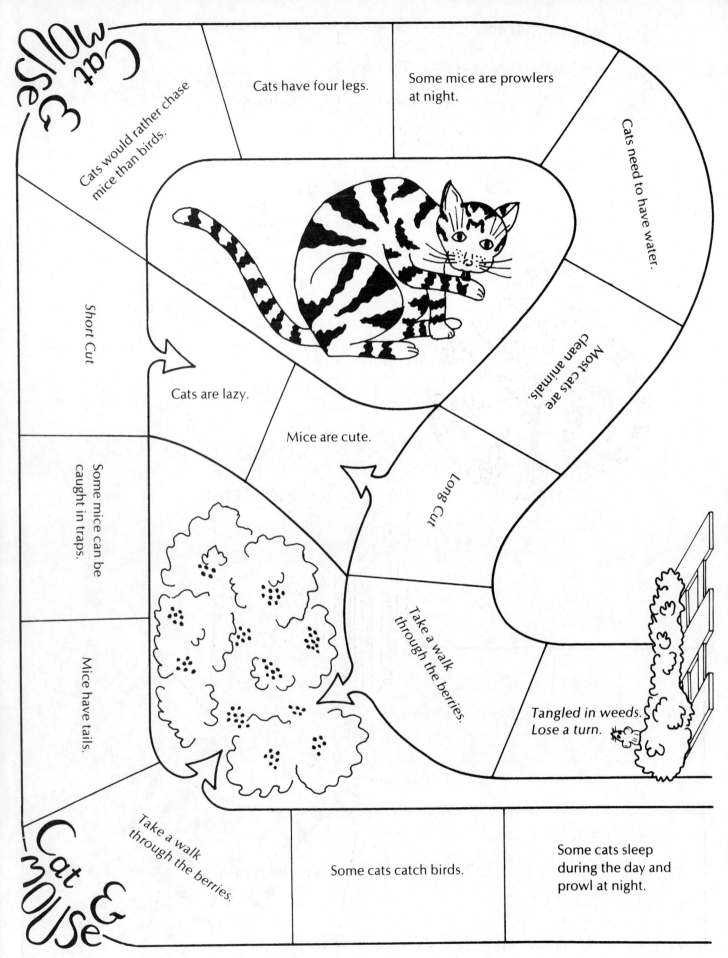

Cats would rather chase mice than birds.

Cats have four legs.

Some mice are prowlers at night.

Cats need to have water.

Short Cut

Most cats are clean animals.

Cats are lazy.

Mice are cute.

Long Cut

Some mice can be caught in traps.

Take a walk through the berries.

Tangled in weeds. Lose a turn.

Mice have tails.

Take a walk through the berries.

Some cats catch birds.

Some cats sleep during the day and prowl at night.

76

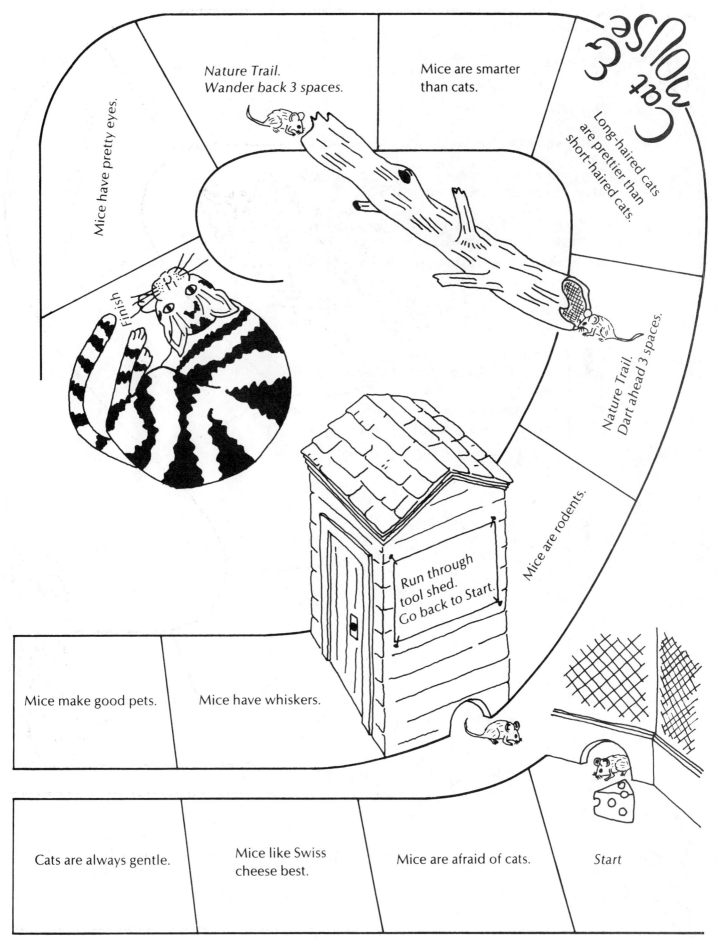

Cat & Mouse

Mice have pretty eyes.

Nature Trail.
Wander back 3 spaces.

Mice are smarter than cats.

Long-haired cats are prettier than short-haired cats.

Finish

Nature Trail. Dart ahead 3 spaces.

Mice are rodents.

Run through tool shed. Go back to Start.

Mice make good pets.

Mice have whiskers.

Cats are always gentle.

Mice like Swiss cheese best.

Mice are afraid of cats.

Start

Quicksand

Purpose   To distinguish fact from opinion in a series of statements.

Number of players   2–4

Materials   Quicksand game board
Deep Water cards
Single die or spinner
Marker for each player

Rules   1   Each player in turn rolls the die or spins and moves his marker the number of spaces shown.

2   If a player lands on a blank space, he has a free turn.

3   If a player lands on a statement, he must tell whether it is fact or opinion. If he answers correctly, he may stay where he landed.

4   If a player answers incorrectly, he must return to his previous position.

5   If a player lands in Deep Water, he draws a Deep Water card and follows the directions.

6   If a player lands in the Quicksand, he loses one turn.

7   The first player to reach Finish is the winner.

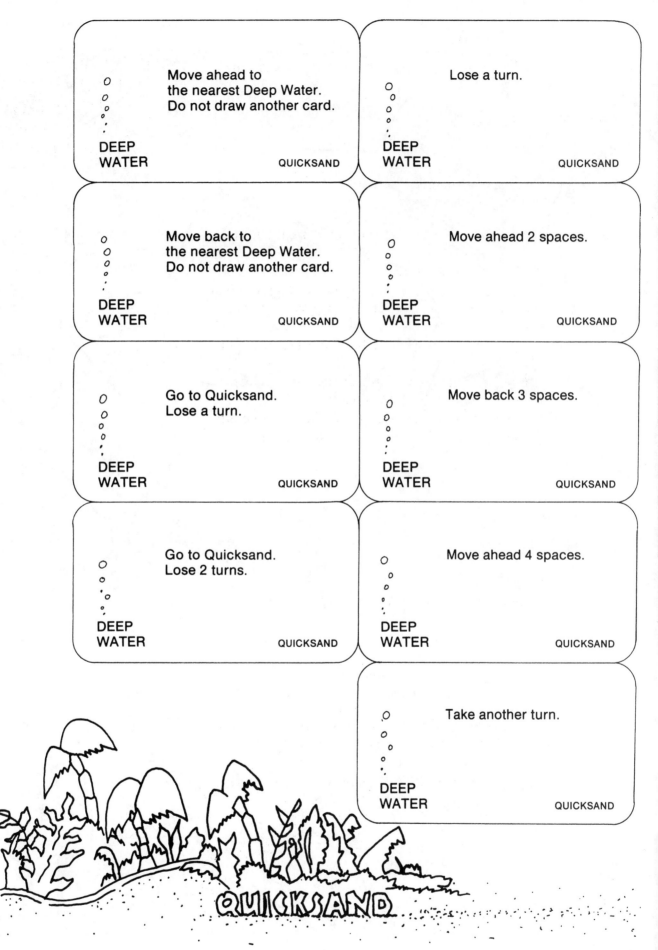

Move ahead to
the nearest Deep Water.
Do not draw another card.

DEEP
WATER

QUICKSAND

Lose a turn.

DEEP
WATER

QUICKSAND

Move back to
the nearest Deep Water.
Do not draw another card.

DEEP
WATER

QUICKSAND

Move ahead 2 spaces.

DEEP
WATER

QUICKSAND

Go to Quicksand.
Lose a turn.

DEEP
WATER

QUICKSAND

Move back 3 spaces.

DEEP
WATER

QUICKSAND

Go to Quicksand.
Lose 2 turns.

DEEP
WATER

QUICKSAND

Move ahead 4 spaces.

DEEP
WATER

QUICKSAND

Take another turn.

DEEP
WATER

QUICKSAND

QUICKSAND

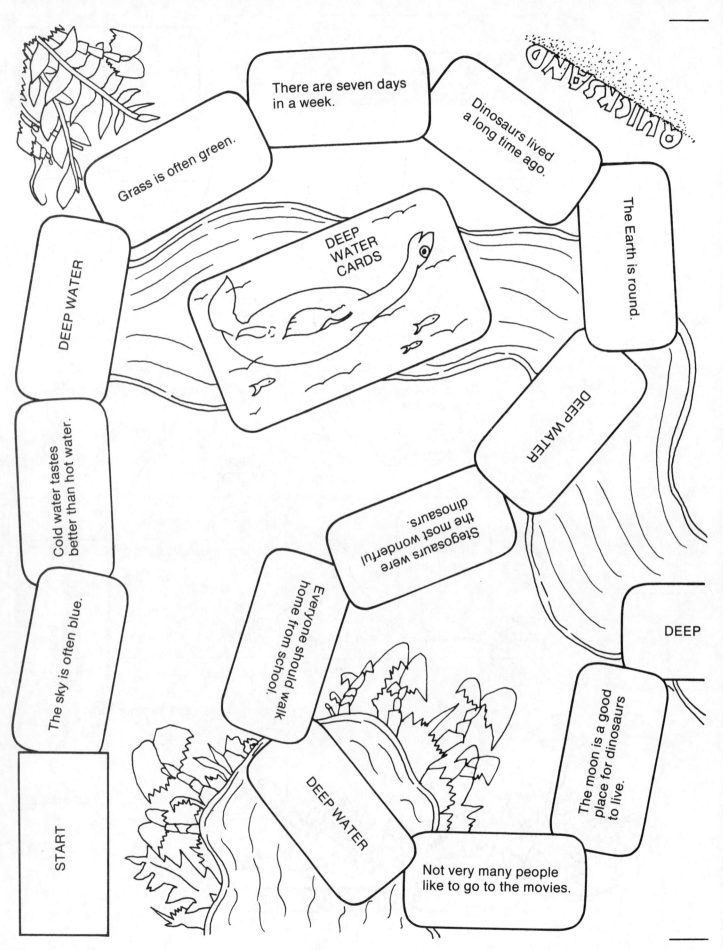

QUICKSAND

There are seven days in a week.

Grass is often green.

Dinosaurs lived a long time ago.

DEEP WATER CARDS

The Earth is round.

DEEP WATER

Cold water tastes better than hot water.

DEEP WATER

Stegosaurs were the most wonderful dinosaurs.

DEEP

The sky is often blue.

Everyone should walk home from school.

The moon is a good place for dinosaurs to live.

START

DEEP WATER

Not very many people like to go to the movies.

80

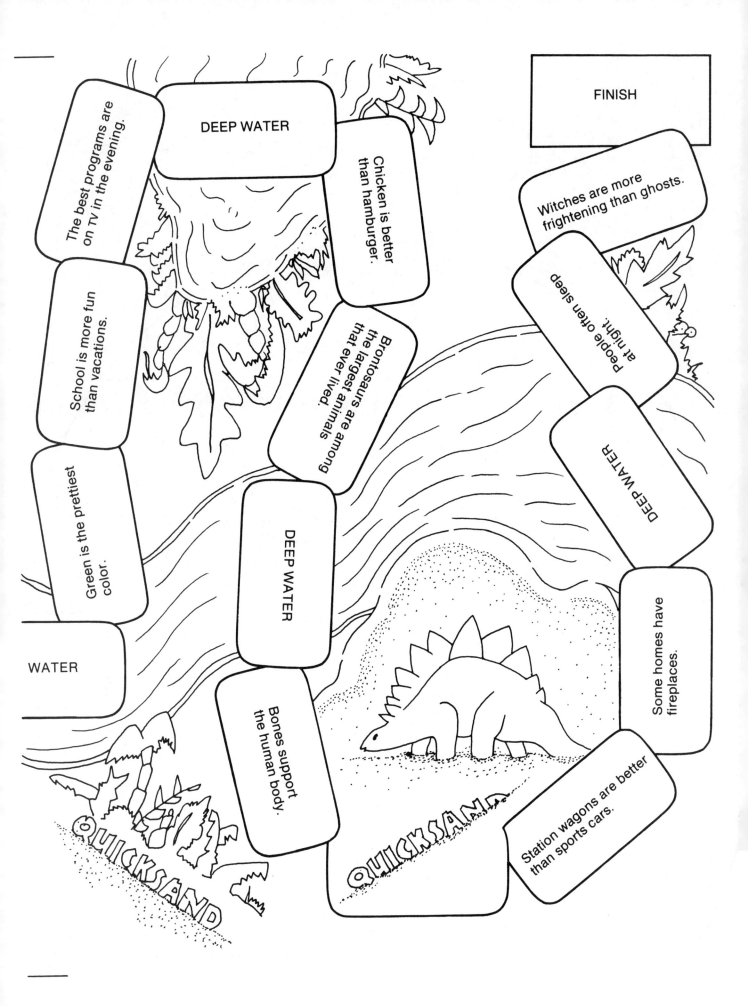

Spinner

Duplicate the spinner, cut it out, and mount it on tagboard. Fasten a brass brad through the center of the spinner, and hook a large paper clip under the head of the brad.

You may want to duplicate a spinner for each game and have it colored or decorated to match the game board.

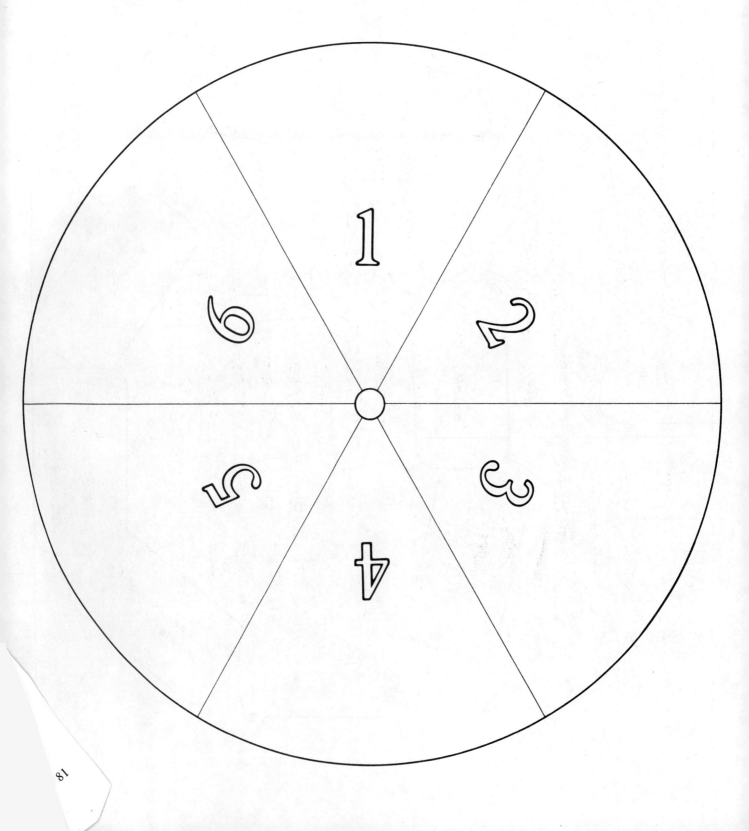